TRUE TO LIFE

PRE-INTERMEDIATE

Ruth Gairns
Stuart Redman

VIDEO ACTIVITY BOOK

CAMBRIDGE
UNIVERSITY PRESS

PUBLISHED BY THE PRESS SYNDICATE OF THE UNIVERSITY OF CAMBRIDGE
The Pitt Building, Trumpington Street, Cambridge, United Kingdom

CAMBRIDGE UNIVERSITY PRESS
The Edinburgh Building, Cambridge CB2 2RU, UK
40 West 20th Street, New York, NY 10011–4211, USA
477 Williamstown Road, Port Melbourne, VIC 3207, Australia
Ruiz de Alarcón 13, 28014 Madrid, Spain
Dock House, The Waterfront, Cape Town 8001, South Africa

http://www.cambridge.org

© Cambridge University Press 1998

First published 1998
Reprinted 2004

Printed in Dubai by Oriental Press

ISBN 0 521 64401 1 True to Life Pre-intermediate Video Activity Book
ISBN 0 521 62894 6 True to Life Pre-intermediate Video VHS PAL
ISBN 0 521 63982 4 True to Life Pre-intermediate Video VHS SECAM
ISBN 0 521 63981 6 True to Life Pre-intermediate Video VHS NTSC

MAP OF THE BOOK

INTRODUCTION

True to Life Pre-intermediate Video is designed to accompany *True to Life Pre-intermediate Class Book*, but it can also be used independently as part of a speaking and listening course, or on its own as a video course.

As a complement to the Class Book, the video provides one sequence for every three Class Book units – Sequence 1 corresponds to Class Book Units 1–3, Sequence 2 to Units 4–6, and so forth. Each video sequence elaborates on a theme from one of the corresponding Class Book units, and offers further practice of grammar and vocabulary from the units. For example, *Line dancing* (Sequence 2) expands on the theme of health and fitness that learners meet in Unit 5 of the Class Book and revises a language point from Unit 4 (infinitive of purpose).

What's in the video?

The video contains eight short documentary sequences, with each one approximately five to eight minutes in length. In some of the sequences we meet two presenters, Katherine and Tyler, who are actors, but all the other speakers are real people interviewed on location in Britain, France and the United States, talking about their lives, their work or their hobbies. They are not reading a prepared script: they all talk naturally and at normal speed, so each sequence does give a snapshot of people's lives which is genuinely true to life.

One sequence in the video which is slightly different is '*Video diary*' (Sequence 5). This was made by Roy Hayes, a businessman, and it records a trip he made to the Czech Republic with his wife for business and pleasure. It was the first video he had ever made, so you will notice some difference in the overall quality of the filming.

What's in the Video Activity Book?

The Video Activity Book provides all the support material for the video, and the wide range of exercises and tasks should provide 60 to 90 minutes of classroom activity for each video sequence. The material for each sequence is divided into the following sections:

Before you watch
The exercises in this section serve to stimulate interest in the theme of the video through short discussion activities, and they often pre-teach important vocabulary from the video.

Watch the video
This is the first opportunity to watch the whole sequence without interruption. There is an accompanying task to help with general understanding but it is not too demanding at this early stage. Sometimes there is a visual element in this task.

Watch again
When learners watch a second time, the sequence is broken down into shorter passages with more detailed comprehension exercises for each one. Again there is sometimes a visual element in some of the exercises, and also some more personalised responses to the video.

After viewing
This section includes grammar and vocabulary exercises, and also more extended personalised speaking activities in which learners discuss different themes related to the video. This section usually concludes with a writing task.

Self study
This is an opportunity for learners to study the tapescript in more detail and, if resources permit, watch the video again. The exercises offer opportunities for vocabulary development, and often include an activity called 'Personal dictation'. In this activity, learners read a short passage from the tapescript several times, then write down key words from the passage, shut their books, and try to reconstruct the text themselves. Afterwards they can compare their text with the tapescript and read aloud the completed passage.

At the back of the book there is an Answer key for the exercises and Tapescripts for all the sequences.

Why use video in the classroom?

For most learners, video is an entertaining and motivating medium. The visual support not only provides valuable assistance in overall comprehension – seeing the gestures and expressions of the speakers and the social content in which they are speaking can be so important – but learners are also usually more interested in what people have to say when they can actually see them. This is, after all, what happens in real life in the majority of situations.

Video also has the capacity to bring the outside world into the classroom with more impact than many audio cassettes or written texts, and it can sometimes generate interest and discussion where other mediums fail. There is the added bonus that video can operate on different levels, stimulating interest through both words and/or pictures.

Video can also convey so much cultural information in a short space of time. For example, the street scenes in *Postcard from Chicago* (Sequence 1) give a strong sense of the energy of a big American city, while the background pictures in *A hotel in France* convey the atmosphere and tranquillity of the hotel and the region in which it is located.

And for many, not the least the teacher, video provides a change of focus. It takes learners away from books and the written word, and introduces variety and a change of pace. Learners enjoy it.

1

POSTCARD FROM CHICAGO

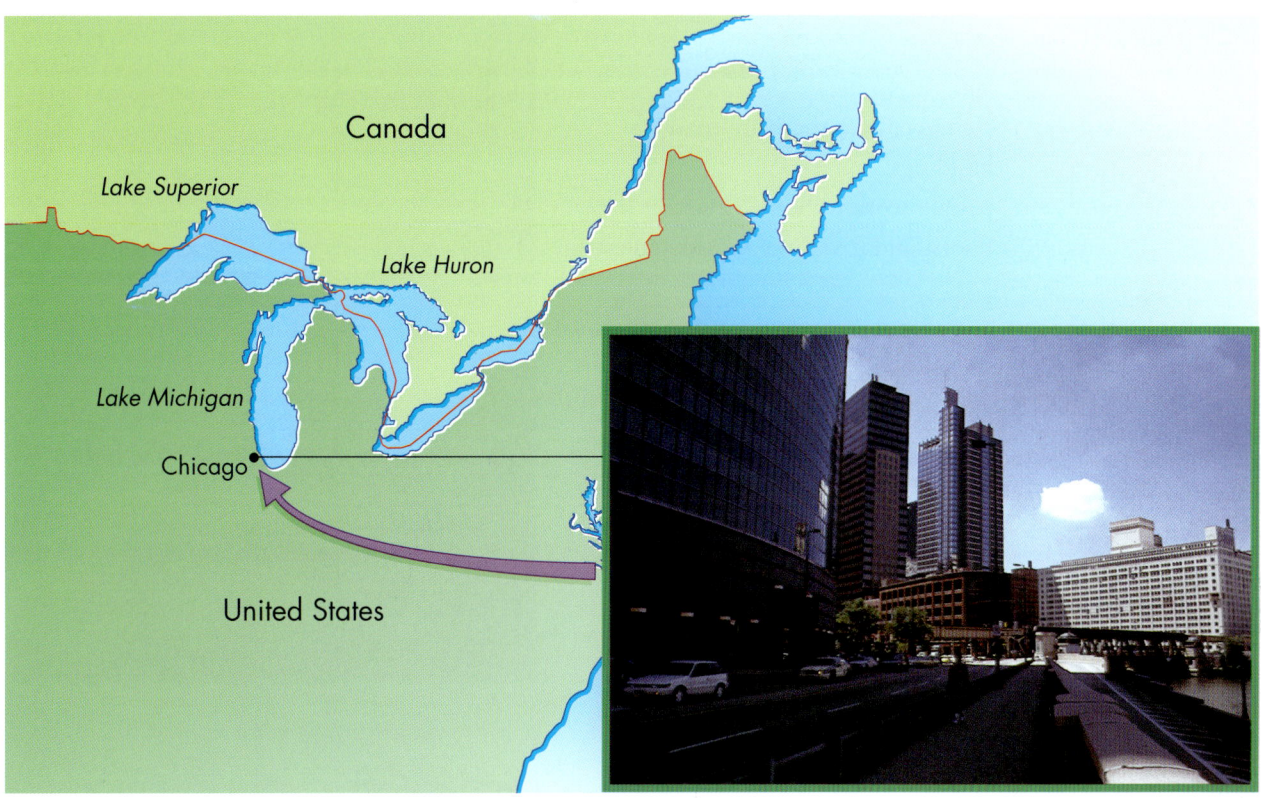

---

1 With a partner, organise these words into four or five groups, and give each one a title, e.g. *types of building*.

museum	river	commercial area	school
taxi cab	factory	high-rise building	fountain
poorer area	hospital	residential area	downtown area
lake	railway	pavement café	restaurant
tram	suburbs	department store	

With your partner, say the words to each other to check you can pronounce each one correctly. With the compound words, you need to pay special attention to the stress.

Example: *commercial* ☐ *area* ☐

WATCH THE VIDEO

2 Watch the video. How many things from Exercise 1 can you see? Tick (✓) the words above as they appear. Compare with a partner.

From your first viewing of the video, what do you think of Chicago? Would you like to go there? Why/why not? Tell your partner.

Background to the city

3 Watch the first section (00:00–00:56) and complete these sentences.

1. Chicago is famous for gangsters, ..., ... and ....
2. In the downtown commercial area there are many .... buildings.
3. .... people work in Sears Tower; it has .... floors, and it was the world's tallest building for ....
4. If you leave the city centre and go to some of the smarter suburbs, you will see beautiful ....
5. They call Frank Lloyd Wright the .... of .... architecture.

Compare with a partner.

Patricia Saldaña Natke

4 Watch the next section (00:57–02:16), and number this information in the order it appears in the video.

Patricia's parents   ☐
Patricia's childhood   ☐
Patricia's job   ☐
Patricia's first project   ☐
Patricia's opinion about architecture ☐

Check with a partner, then watch the section again. What do you learn about each of these five subjects? Tell your partner.

Life in the city

5 Watch the final section of the video (02:17–04:03). Answer these questions.

1. What kind of restaurants do you see?
2. What kind of music do you hear?

There is also a scene where Patricia orders a pizza. Underline the exact phrases used from these choices. The first one has been done for you.

WAITRESS:		
Hi there. How are you today?		
PATRICIA:		
Good, thank you.	OR	Fine, thanks.
WAITRESS:		
Good. What would you like?	OR	Great. What can I get you?
PATRICIA:		
I'll have a sausage and mushroom pizza.	OR	Could I have a sausage and mushroom pizza?
WAITRESS:		
OK. What size on that?	OR	OK. Large or small?
PATRICIA:		
Small, please.	OR	Small.
WAITRESS:		
Small. And to drink?	OR	Small. What can I get you to drink?
PATRICIA:		
I'll have a coke.	OR	A small coke.
WAITRESS:		
A small coke. All right, I'll be right back out with your drink.	OR	Thanks, I'll go and get your drink.

Compare your answers with your partner and then the tapescript on page 55, then look at the dialogue again. This time, practise the dialogue using the other phrases. Continue until you can do it without looking at your book, both as Patricia and the waitress.

Language note

One or two of the phrases used in the dialogue on the video are examples of American English, and are not common in British English. They are:
1. The reply 'Good, thank you'. The usual British response to 'How are you?' is 'Fine, thank you'.
2. The question 'What size on that?' In a similar situation, most British speakers would ask 'What size (would you like)?'

Grammar and speaking – past simple

6 Complete the text using suitable verbs in the past simple tense.

Patricia (1) ...... *was born* ...... in Mexico, but when she (2) .... a baby her parents (3) .... to Chicago and that is where she (4) .... She lived in a poor area called the Stockyards. She (5) .... well at school and (6) .... to university, where she (7) .... architecture. When she (8) .... she managed to get a job with Urban Works. Her first project (9) .... a school in the Stockyards area.

Practise reading the text aloud, then tell your partner about *your* background.

Speaking

7 In the video, Patricia says that 'beautiful architecture has a very positive effect on people'. What other features of towns can have a very positive effect on people or a very negative effect on people? Work in small groups and make two lists.

Positive	*Negative*
e.g. parks	e.g. litter
....	....
....	....
....	....
....	....
....	....
....	....
....	....

Compare and discuss your lists with another group.

Writing

8 You are going to write an introduction to your city, similar to the introduction at the beginning of the unit and on the video. Use the following framework and complete the gaps.

This is .... It is located in the .... of .... , and has approximately .... inhabitants. .... is famous for .... and .... , and we get .... tourists. The transport system is .... and most people travel around by .... For entertainment, people ....

Writing and speaking

9 Complete one half of this restaurant dialogue in a suitable way and then compare with a partner.

WAITER: Are you ready to order?

CUSTOMER: ....

WAITER: Right. What ....?

CUSTOMER: I think I ....

WAITER: And .... salad or french fries with that?

CUSTOMER: Yeah, ..., please.

WAITER: OK. And what ....?

CUSTOMER: .... beer.

WAITER: Fine. I'll bring your drink now.

CUSTOMER: ....

Practise the dialogue with your partner several times. Change the food and drink you order each time.

SELF STUDY

Personal dictation

1 Read the first paragraph from the tapescript spoken by the narrator (the underlined section on page 55). Read it aloud two or three times, so you are very familiar with it.

Read it once more, and write down not more than 12 important words in the paragraph.

Shut your book, and try to write down what the narrator says. It needn't be exactly the same, but must contain the main information. When you have finished, compare what you wrote with the tapescript.

Word puzzle

2 You will find all the words in the puzzle in the tapescript for this lesson on page 55. When you have finished, the letters in the black box will spell another word.

1. Used to describe light or colours, it means *strong* and *easy to see.*
2. Often used as the opposite of *old* or *old-fashioned.*
3. This word can mean *big* but in the video it means *fantastic.*
4. Used to describe someone or something that is well-known.
5. Can mean the same as *lucky.*
6. If you 'produce' a lot, you are this.
7. The person or thing you like most is this.
8. It means *very, very big.*
9. It can mean *beautiful, graceful* and *smart.*

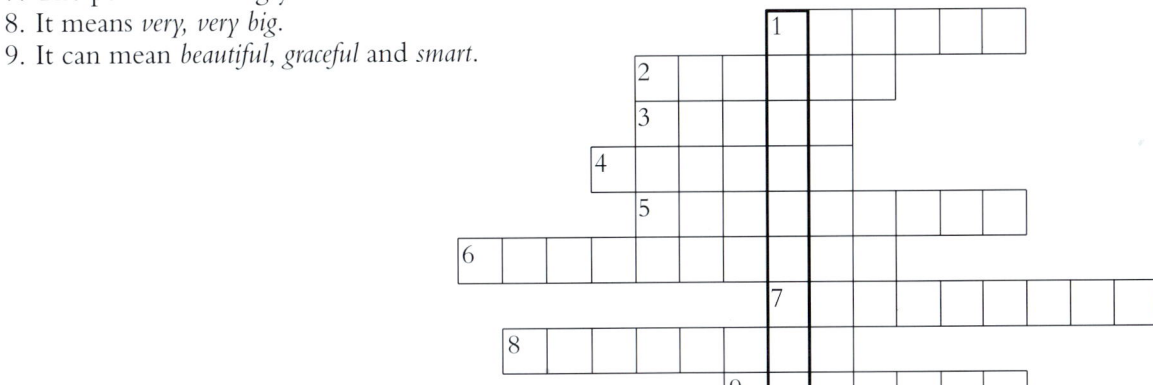

LINE DANCING

1 Discuss the questions in the box in small groups.

> **How do you spend your evening leisure time?**
>
> 1. In your country, what *organised* leisure activities are there for people to do in the evenings? (For example, aerobics classes, chess clubs ...)
> 2. Where do these activities usually take place? (For example, in a school building.)
> 3. Do people learn to dance in the evenings? If so, what kinds of dance do they learn? Have you ever been to a dancing class?
> 4. If you are single★, which particular leisure activities can you do *with other people*?

Language note

★ *single*: with no husband, wife or long-term partner

rock and roll

ballroom dancing

disco dancing

2 You are going to watch a video about line dancing. Read these questions first.

1. What do you learn about line dancing?
2. What kind of building are they using?
3. In your country, do you think line dancing would be popular?
4. If so, what kind of building would they use?

Now watch the video and discuss your answers in small groups.

Heather teaches Tyler to dance

3 **A** Match the instructions with the pictures, then compare with a partner.

1. step out to the right
2. hook behind with your left
3. walk backward(s)
4. turn

5. clap
6. go forward(s)
7. slide
8. touch the ground

Now cover the words and look at the pictures. With your partner, see if you can remember the instructions.

B Watch the lesson Heather gives (05:12–06:45), and complete the gaps in her instructions.

HEATHER: Right, OK, first of all, if you'd like to put your hands behind your back or you can put your hands in the front of your jeans.

TYLER: } Oh, right. Yeah, I'll, I'll do that, shall I. All right, yeah.

HEATHER: } And just let your arms be relaxed. And then the first step that we're gonna do is called a 'grapevine'. So you (1) .... to the right, [yeah] behind with your left, [yeah] out to the right [yeah] and a touch, OK?

TYLER: A touch with? OK.

HEATHER: Just a touch with the left. Then you're going to go back and do exactly the same, [all right] step out with the left, (2) ...., out with the left, with a touch for the right.

TYLER: Right, OK.

HEATHER: That is called a 'grapevine' step.

TYLER: } That step, all right.

HEATHER: } OK, OK let's go from the beginning and ... out, behind, out with a touch, and left behind, left with a touch.

TYLER: Great.

HEATHER: Got it?

HEATHER/TYLER: Right, left, right, hook, (3) ....

HEATHER: Bend your knees and hook behind with your right. OK, let's do that together, then, walking backward first of all. And back, two, three, (4) ....! Forward, hook, back, hook, step, (5) ...., step, turn, grapevine. Go straight into that. You have to turn.

TYLER: Oh, yes.

HEATHER: There is a movement [yeah?], carry on dancing, I can show you, as you (6) ...., you can touch the floor. [Oh!] Stretch your arms and (7) .... [OK], and back, two, three, four, forward, touch, back and step, side, step ... to make it more fun.

TYLER: (*laughing*) Right! OK.

Now it's your turn. Stand up, make a space, play the video again, and follow Heather's instructions.

Why do people do it?

4 Look at the questions in the box and check that you understand the vocabulary.

Who does it ...
– to keep fit? .... *Barbara* ....
– to have a laugh? ....
– to lose weight? ....
– because it's great fun? ....
– because you don't need a partner? ....
– because you don't have to be very good at it? ....
– because the time goes so quickly? ....

Andrew

Rhona

Barbara

Julie

Watch the video (06:47–08:19) and write the correct name next to each question.

Is line dancing easy or difficult?

5 Watch the video (08:20–09:38) and write T (true) or F (false) next to each sentence, according to what the speakers say.

1. Some line dancing is similar to ballroom dancing. ☐
2. One person thinks that younger people learn quicker than older people. ☐
3. It gives you mental exercise. ☐
4. Men learn more slowly than women. ☐

How good is the teacher?

6 Watch the video (09:39–11:05). What do the students think of their teacher, Heather? How many things do you remember?

Grammar and speaking – infinitive of purpose

7 Look at these examples:

*Barbara goes line dancing **to keep fit**.*
*Rhona goes line dancing **to have a laugh**.*

You can use the infinitive (*to* + verb) to give the reason for doing something, to say *why* you do something.

Why do people go to these places? With a partner, think of at least two reasons for each one.

Example: Why do people go to discos?
            to meet people, to have fun, to dance, to have a drink …

libraries	parks	chess clubs	parties
the beach	football matches	banks	airports

Find another pair and compare your answers.

Speaking

8 Choose one or two of the following activities to do in small groups.

> Do you think line dancing is easy or difficult? Why?
> Are there other kinds of dancing that are easier, or more difficult? Think of examples.
> Are there physical sports which are easier/more difficult than line dancing? Which and why?

> The people in the video think Heather is a very good teacher. What about you?
> Would you like Heather as a dance teacher? Why/why not?
> Do you think dance teachers should be different from teachers of other subjects? Why/why not?

> Do you know a dance that other people in your group can't do? Teach them some steps of the dance, but first think about the instructions in English.

Writing

9 Choose A or B.

A Look at the pictures in Exercise 3. Without looking at the vocabulary, write out the instructions for each picture.

B Think of the four simple steps of the 'grapevine' step that Heather taught Tyler: four steps to one side, then four steps back.

Work with a partner. Can you invent a little dance like that? Plan it together. You probably need to *do* your dance, so stand up!

Now write the instructions clearly. When you have finished, give them to another pair. Can they do your dance?

SELF STUDY

Personal dictation

1 Read the underlined section of the tapescript on page 56. If necessary, check any new words in a dictionary.

Read it aloud two or three times, to help you remember it.

Read it once more, and write down not more than 12 important words in the interview.

Shut your book, and try to write down what the presenter says. It needn't be exactly the same, but must contain the main information. When you have finished, compare what you wrote with the tapescript.

Vocabulary

2 Match the verbs on the left with a word or phrase on the right.

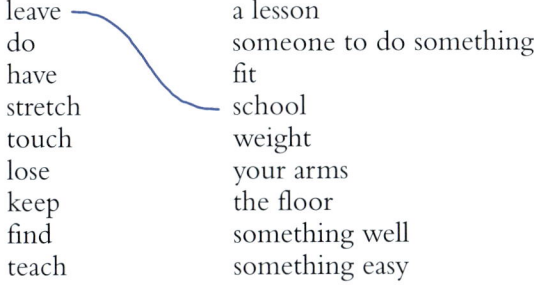

leave	a lesson
do	someone to do something
have	fit
stretch	school
touch	weight
lose	your arms
keep	the floor
find	something well
teach	something easy

The phrases above are all in the tapescript on page 56. Go through it and underline them.

3

A HOTEL IN FRANCE

1 A In a hotel, what do these members of staff★ do? Discuss with a partner.

- waiters/waitresses
- bar staff
- chefs
- chambermaids
- receptionists

Language note

★ *staff*: people who work for an organisation, especially in a hotel, restaurant, school, etc.

Who are the guests, and what do they do?

B Match the words with the pictures, and check that you can pronounce them correctly.

olives	garlic	cold meat	salami	roast beef and Yorkshire pudding
cereals	steak	cabbage	croissant	French bread/baguette

2 You are now thinking about your next holiday. Watch the video about a hotel in Fayence in the South of France. Is it the kind of hotel you would like to stay in? Why/why not?

Wolf Rilla   Shirley Rilla

The hotel

3 Watch the first section (11:17–13:01) again, and complete the summary.

Wolf and Shirley Rilla opened the hotel (1) .... years ago. They wanted to create a hotel that was more (2) .... than the big five-star hotels. The rooms are (3) .... the same size: the smaller rooms cost about (4) .... francs per person including (5) .... and (6) ....; the de luxe apartment costs about (7) .... francs per person. Altogether, the hotel has (8) .... rooms and Wolf and Shirley try to make them as (9) .... as possible.

The guests

4 Watch the next section (13:02–13:54) and answer the questions.

1. Which people come to the hotel for a weekend break?
2. Who comes at the beginning and end of the season?
3. Who comes in July and August?
4. Which guests always enjoy themselves?
5. Which guests are very amusing?

Food in different cultures

5 A Watch the next section (13:55–16:36) without the sound. With a partner, name all the food and drinks you see.

B Watch the section again (with the sound) and choose the best answer in italics.

1. Shirley likes cooking *roast beef and Yorkshire pudding/classic French food* for the guests.
2. The Dutch usually have *a three-course meal/a sandwich* for lunch.
3. The Americans often want *coffee/milk* with their meals.
4. The Americans ask for their steak *medium/well done*.
5. *The English/the Americans* always ask for sugar-free cereals.
6. The Dutch and Germans generally prefer *cold meat/cereals* for breakfast.

What do you think of the answers to questions 2–6? For example, do people in your country have a sandwich for lunch or have coffee with their meals? Discuss in groups.

Rules

6 Watch the last section (16:37–17:38) and complete Shirley and Wolf's rules for new members of staff employed at the hotel.

You must be ....

You must be ....

You mustn't be ....

Remember! The customer is ....

Visual quiz

7 With your partner, make lists of what you can remember:

– four things you saw the staff doing
– four things you saw the guests doing
– any furniture/objects you saw in the bedrooms
– four things you saw on the breakfast table (not food or drinks)

Compare your lists with the class.

Grammar and speaking – modal verbs of obligation

8 Read these rules of an imaginary hotel, using a dictionary if necessary.

Do you agree with them? Discuss in groups and, if necessary, change the sentences to make rules that you agree with.

Example: Guests *cannot* bring dogs into the hotel or garden.
Your rules:
Guests can bring dogs into the garden, but not into the hotel.
Guests can bring dogs into the hotel and garden but mustn't leave them alone in the bedrooms.

● Guests *cannot* bring dogs into the hotel or garden.

● Waiters *have to* wear a uniform at all times.

● Guests *don't have to* dress smartly for dinner.

● At the end of their stay, guests *have to* leave their rooms before 10.00 in the morning.

● Chambermaids *must* put clean sheets on the beds every day.

● Guests *must not* take other visitors into their bedrooms.

● Waiters *should* always serve women before men at the same table.

● Guests *cannot* smoke in the restaurant.

● If guests are rude* to waiters, the waiters *must* always be polite to guests.

● The reception staff *don't have to* show guests to their room when they first arrive.

Language note

★ *rude*: not polite

Writing

9 Imagine you are staying at the hotel in the video. You have been there three days and you are going to write a postcard to an English friend in your home town.

You could write about:
- the weather
- the hotel
- the food
- the service
- the place
- what you have done so far on your holiday

Personal dictation

1 Read what Shirley and Wolf say about the staff they employ, the underlined section of the tapescript on page 57. If necessary, check any new words in a dictionary.

> **Language note**
>
> ★ *a complaint*: if you make a complaint in a hotel, you tell the staff that you are unhappy about something, like the service, or perhaps your room is too noisy

Read it aloud two or three times, to help you remember it.

Read it once more, and write down not more than 12 important words in the interview.

Shut your book, and try to write down what Shirley and Wolf say. It needn't be exactly the same, but must contain the main information. When you have finished, compare what you wrote with the tapescript.

Vocabulary

2 Complete these phrases using the tapescript.

half an .... *hour* ....   a de luxe ....

a three-course ....   the night before ....

a five-star ....

Now change the first part of each phrase in a suitable way.

Example: half an hour   *a quarter of an hour*

CHESTER ZOO

1 Complete these sentences about people and animals, then discuss in small groups, giving your reasons.

1. The animal I would most like to have is a ....
2. I think animals are (more) .... than people.
3. I feel that eating animal meat is ....
4. Going to see animals in a zoo is ....

2 A Match the pictures with the words, and make sure you can pronounce them.

| snake | chimp (chimpanzee) | camel | deer | elephant | giraffe | lemur |
| tiger | gorilla | lion | bear | kangaroo | orang-utan | |

B Complete the table, using a dictionary if necessary.

Nouns	Adjectives
aggression	aggressive
....	happy
....	strong
....	popular
....	noisy
....	timid
dominance	....
intelligence	....
smell	....

Work in small groups. Use the adjectives to describe the animals in the photos.

Example: *I think deer are usually very timid.*

3 Before you watch the video, check that you understand the verbs in italics in the box below.

someone *touching* a snake ☐
a chimpanzee *cuddling* its baby ☐
a lemur *carrying* a baby on its back ☐
a chimp *throwing* another chimp into the air ☐
a keeper★ *feeding* animals ☐
a giraffe *biting* another giraffe ☐
one chimp *cleaning/grooming* another ☐
a chimp *clapping* ☐
a snake *attacking* someone or something ☐

Language note

★ *keeper*: a person who looks after animals: zoo keeper, snake keeper

Now watch the video and tick the activities in the box above that you see.

Compare with a partner.

WATCH AGAIN

Snakes

4 Watch the interview with the snake keeper (18:28–19:33) and correct the five mistakes in the tapescript below.

KATHERINE: A lot of people are scared of snakes. I'm quite scared of snakes. This is Keith. He looks after the snakes at the zoo. Can I cuddle it?

SNAKE KEEPER: You certainly can. This is an African king snake. They're called king snakes because they actually attack and eat rattlesnakes. Many people know a great deal about snakes. When you work with them, if you look at them, people say how can you tell that they're happy, mad, sick or healthy★. I've worked with snakes for over 30 years. I can just look at them and I know by their behaviour whether they're happy, sad or angry. And even this is a very, very placid★ snake, but if he was upset or frightened, he would bite you.

KATHERINE: Really?

SNAKE KEEPER: Really.

Language note

★ *healthy*: physically strong and well
★ *placid*: calm, quiet; doesn't get excited or aggressive

Lemurs

5 Read the sentences below, then watch
the section on lemurs (19:51–21:35)
and complete the sentences.

1. A family of lemurs usually has
   .... members.

2. The head animal is
   ....

3. The females★ usually eat ....

4. Some lemurs are aggressive and some
   ....

5. The keeper thinks you can have a stronger
   relationship with ....

Chimps

6 Watch the interview with the chimp keeper (21:50–24:18). He talks about the four
subjects in the boxes. Make notes, then compare with a partner. Watch twice if necessary.

How chimps are similar to people

A chimp called Boris

A chimp called Nicky

The character of chimps

Grammar – superlatives

7 Complete the table.

Adjective	Superlative
big	*the biggest*
intelligent	*the most intelligent*
small	
tall	
frightening	
strong	
fast	
dangerous	
strange	
friendly	
beautiful	

With a partner, look at the pictures in Exercise 1. Use the superlative forms above to talk about the animals.

Example: *Elephants are the biggest, and I think chimps are probably the most intelligent.*

Notice that we use *elephants* and *chimps* with a plural verb and no article to talk about animals in general.

Writing

8 Imagine you are Katherine and you spent the day at Chester Zoo.
Write a short account about what you did and saw.

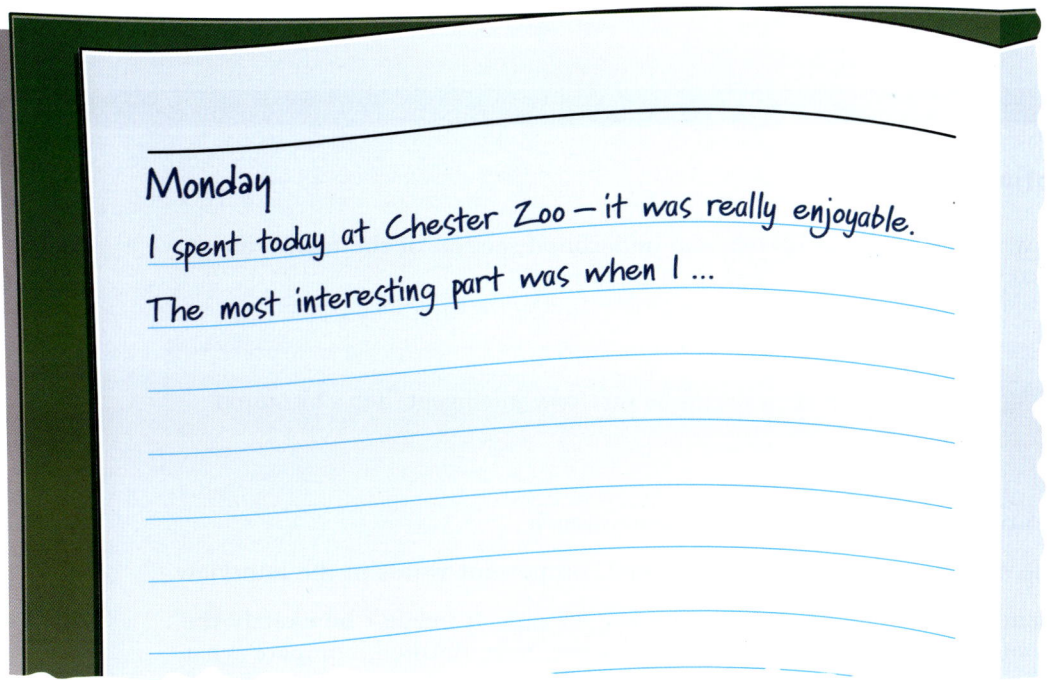

Monday
I spent today at Chester Zoo – it was really enjoyable.
The most interesting part was when I ...

Speaking

9 Look at the pictures in Exercise 1. With a partner, imagine you are zoo keepers, and choose one animal you would like to look after. Think about:

– what you like about them
– how easy or difficult they are to look after
– what you have to do when you are looking after them
– what kind of food they like
– what their character is like
– how similar they are to humans

Now find a new partner. Interview them about the animal they have chosen to look after. Make questions from the ideas in the box above.

Example: *What do you like about (camels)?*
Are they easy to look after? Why?

Personal dictation

1 Read the interview with the chimp keeper, the underlined section of the tapescript on page 58. If necessary, check any new words in a dictionary.

> **Language note**
>
> ★ Nicky is *a bit thick*: this is colloquial; it means he isn't very intelligent, he's a bit stupid

Read it aloud two or three times, to help you remember it.

Read it once more, and write down not more than 12 important words in the interview.

Shut your book, and try to write down what the keeper says. It needn't be exactly the same, but must contain the main information. When you have finished, compare what you wrote with the tapescript.

Word snake

2 Enter the answers to the clues in the snake. The last letter of each answer is also the first letter of the next answer.

Example: TABL**E**XCELLEN**T**ENNI**S**PEN**D**OO**R** ...

The blue squares show the end/beginning letters of words. The first two clues have been done for you.

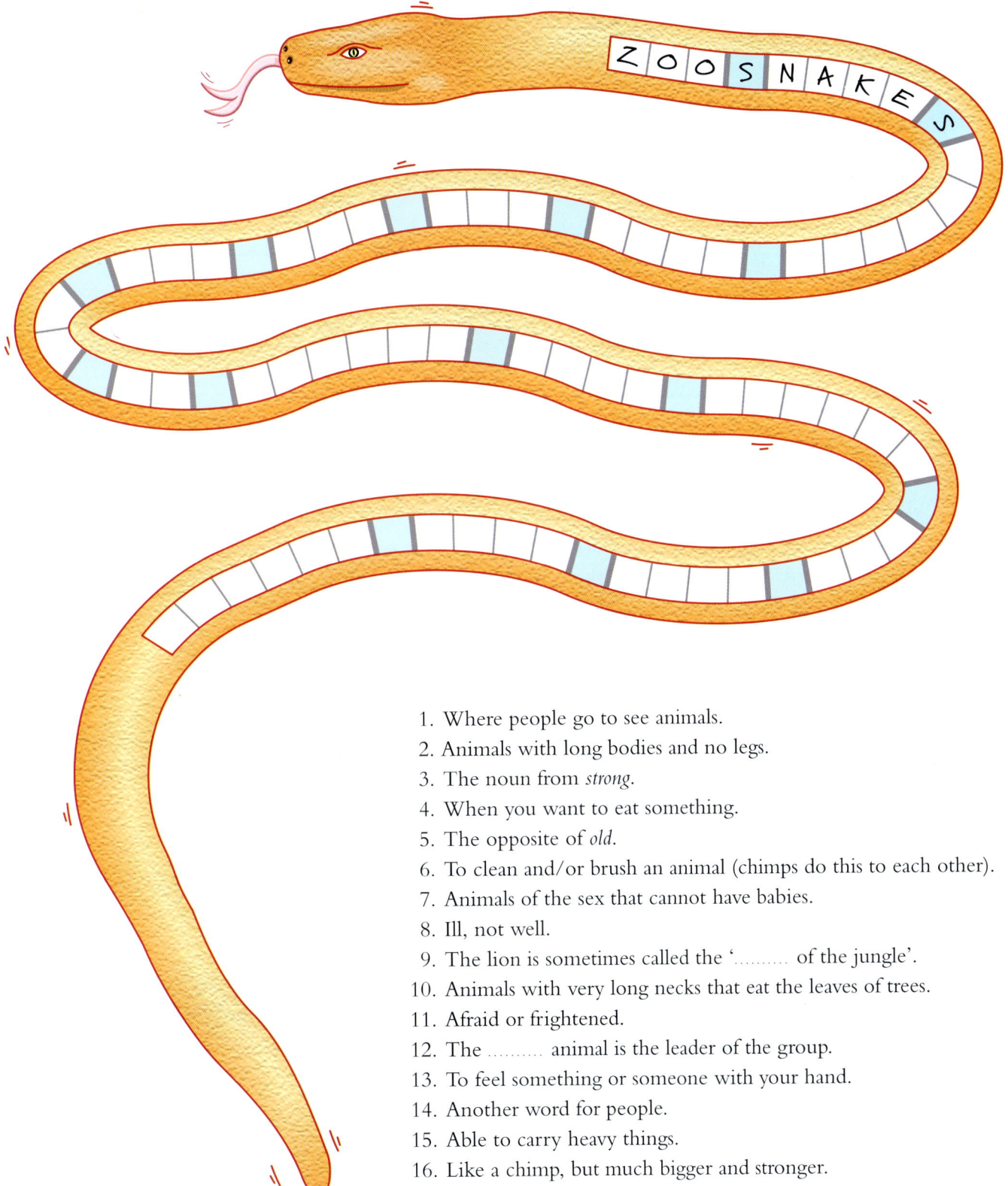

1. Where people go to see animals.
2. Animals with long bodies and no legs.
3. The noun from *strong*.
4. When you want to eat something.
5. The opposite of *old*.
6. To clean and/or brush an animal (chimps do this to each other).
7. Animals of the sex that cannot have babies.
8. Ill, not well.
9. The lion is sometimes called the '.......... of the jungle'.
10. Animals with very long necks that eat the leaves of trees.
11. Afraid or frightened.
12. The .... animal is the leader of the group.
13. To feel something or someone with your hand.
14. Another word for people.
15. Able to carry heavy things.
16. Like a chimp, but much bigger and stronger.

5

VIDEO DIARY: A TRIP TO THE CZECH REPUBLIC

— camcorder

1 A Read the text and say if the statements below are true or false.

A **video diary** is a video you make about something happening in your life. It could be a holiday diary, or preparing for a wedding or the wedding itself. People often do it as a souvenir of a special day, but it can also be just a normal event in your life; for example, a family discussion, giving your dog a bath, opening birthday presents. You can then make a voice recording to say what is happening.

In Britain, the BBC recently had the idea of giving some ordinary people a camcorder so that they could make a short video diary. The technical quality of the filming is not perfect, but these two-minute videos are shown on TV once a week and they are often very interesting stories of moments in people's lives.

1. Video diaries can sometimes be seen on TV in Britain.
2. They are technically of a very high standard.
3. They can be about a special event or an everyday event.
4. They often tell a story.

B Work in small groups, and discuss the questions below.

1. Have you got a camcorder?
2. If so, have you ever done anything like this?
3. If so, what did you film?
4. If you haven't got a camcorder, would you like to have one and make video diaries?

Roy and Irena Hayes

2 Roy Hayes lives near Cambridge and works as an export manager for a company selling animal feed★ to farmers★. He and his wife, Irena, went on a trip to the Czech Republic and they made a video diary.

> **Language note**
>
> ★ *animal feed*: food for farm animals
> ★ *farmers*: people who work on or own farms, where they grow things or keep animals such as cows, sheep, chickens

First read the sentences and check that you understand them. Then watch the video and number the sentences in the order they appear in the video.

They checked into a hotel. □
They went to visit his father-in-law. □
He gave a presentation to clients. □
They went out for a meal with some clients. □
They went sightseeing in Prague. □
He did his packing. □
He looked around a farm. □
They went to see some old friends. □

The journey out and starting business

3 Watch the first section of the video (24:30–26:41) and answer these questions. Watch twice if necessary.

1. When and where did Roy meet his wife?
2. Why does he prefer travelling by car?
3. What does Irena think about British drivers?
4. What does Roy think about Czech drivers?
5. What does Roy do with clients after a meeting?
6. How does he get on with his clients?

Enjoying themselves on a farm and in Prague

4 In the next section of the video (26:42–29:08), Roy and Irena visit friends and go sightseeing. Look at the words and phrases in the box, check that you understand them, then try to identify all of them on the video.

a toy doll	play in the sand	drink a toast
shake hands with someone	hug someone	feed the geese (*large birds*)
kiss someone	have a barbecue	cook sardines (*a type of fish*)

Now watch the section again, but this time you are going to turn down the sound and do the commentary yourself. Work with a partner. As you watch, tell your partner what is happening. You can repeat this with your partner telling you what is happening.

It starts like this:

They are driving through the countryside.
Now they are arriving at the farm.
A cat is ...

Back to business

5 A Watch the next section of the video (29:09–30:28) and complete this text. (Each blank is one word or a short phrase.)

Monday, and I had to get out of .... mode and back into .... mode. I've never been very good .... I do speak a bit of Czech but Irena tells me my ...., so I get an interpreter along to .... I used to get really nervous about ...., but I'm now pretty confident and actually ....

B In the part where Roy gives a presentation, note down everything that people are doing.

Example: *Roy is using an OHP (overhead projector).*

Roy's father-in-law and the journey home

6 Watch the final section of the video (30:29–32:05) and answer these questions.

1. What do you learn about Roy's father-in-law?
2. What did Roy feel about the whole trip?
3. What did he feel about getting home?

Speaking

7 Work with a partner, and act out the first roleplay.

A: You are Roy.
You meet your neighbour when you get home from the Czech Republic.
B: You are Roy's neighbour.
You are going to ask Roy about his trip to the Czech Republic. First look at these two examples of questions you might ask, then think of four or five more.

Examples: *When did you get home?*
Did you have a good time?

When you have finished, act out the second roleplay.

A: You are Irena's neighbour.
You meet her when she returns from her trip to the Czech Republic. First, think of some questions to ask her, as in the first roleplay.
B: You are Irena.
You will have to think about the days when Roy was working. What did you do on those days?

Grammar – adjective + preposition

8 Find the best sentence ending on the right for each of the sentence beginnings on the left, and fill in the missing preposition from this list.

> for   on (2)   in   at   about   as   by

I would like a job	...*on*... a farm when I was younger.
I hardly ever go out	.... learning languages.
I lived	.... a manager of a large company.
I often go	.... a quiet village.
I'm not confident	.... business trips.
I'm not good	.... speaking English.
I love travelling	.... a meal in the evenings.
I would love to live	.... plane.

Look at the sentences again. How many of them are true for you? Discuss in small groups, and give reasons for your answers if you can.

Writing

9 This was Roy's first video diary. Imagine you are going to write him a short letter about it. First think about these questions.

1. What was your general impression of the Czech Republic?
2. Which part did you find most interesting?
3. What would you like to make a video of?

Now write your own letter to Roy or complete this one in a suitable way.

Dear Roy

I have just seen your video diary of the Czech Republic, and I thought it was .... I have never been to the Czech Republic, so it was .... and Prague looked .... I think my favourite part was .... I don't have a camcorder but I would very much like to make a video of .... I'm sure it's more difficult than it looks. Thanks again, and good luck with your next video diary.

Best wishes

....

Reading and reading aloud

1 Here is an early part of Roy's video diary. The sentences are in the wrong order;
number them in the right order, then compare with the tapescript on page 59.

Irena is Czech, and we met when I was on a business trip there a few years ago. ☐

She thinks British people drive too fast; I think Czech people drive too slowly. ☐

The only problem is that Irena and I can never agree who should drive. ☐

I prefer travelling by car because you get to see the countryside and you can stop when you want. ☐

I don't like aeroplanes, so I always go by car. ☐

I went to the Czech Republic with my wife, Irena. ☐

Now practise reading aloud the reordered text. Keep reading it until you can
say it without looking.

2 The tapescript has a lot of very useful phrases. You can use these to say many
different things.

Example: *It was really nice to* see some old friends.

.spend some time in the country. ....

.walk round the old town. ....

Now complete these useful phrases (*in italics*) in different ways.

1. *What I like about* the city *is* the architecture.

....

....

2. If you go on a business trip,
it's a good chance to   buy lots of presents.

....

....

3. *Most of my work involves*   meeting existing clients.

....

....

4. *We always go out for*   a meal.

....

....

5. *I learnt the word for*   'sardines'.

....

....

6. *I've never been very good at*   learning languages.

....

....

6

CREATING SPECIAL EFFECTS

BEFORE YOU WATCH

1 Read these definitions. Make sure you understand them because they are very important to your understanding of the video.

Animatronics is the creation of models of people or animals, which are electrically operated and can move in different ways so they look almost real.

A **prosthetic** is a piece of artificial flesh or skin. First you make this piece of flesh or skin, then artists can put special effects on it to make people look older or ugly, etc. In other words it is a very advanced kind of make-up.

Read these questions. Make sure you understand the meaning of the words in bold, then answer them. Discuss your answers in small groups.

1. Can you think of a **feature film** which uses a lot of **special effects**?
2. Who is the **star** of this film?
3. Who is the **director**?
4. What is the film about?

WATCH THE VIDEO

2 Look at the pictures below, then watch the video and answer these questions.

1. Who is Pauline Fowler?
2. What's happening to Katherine?
3. Why are these three creatures in the video?

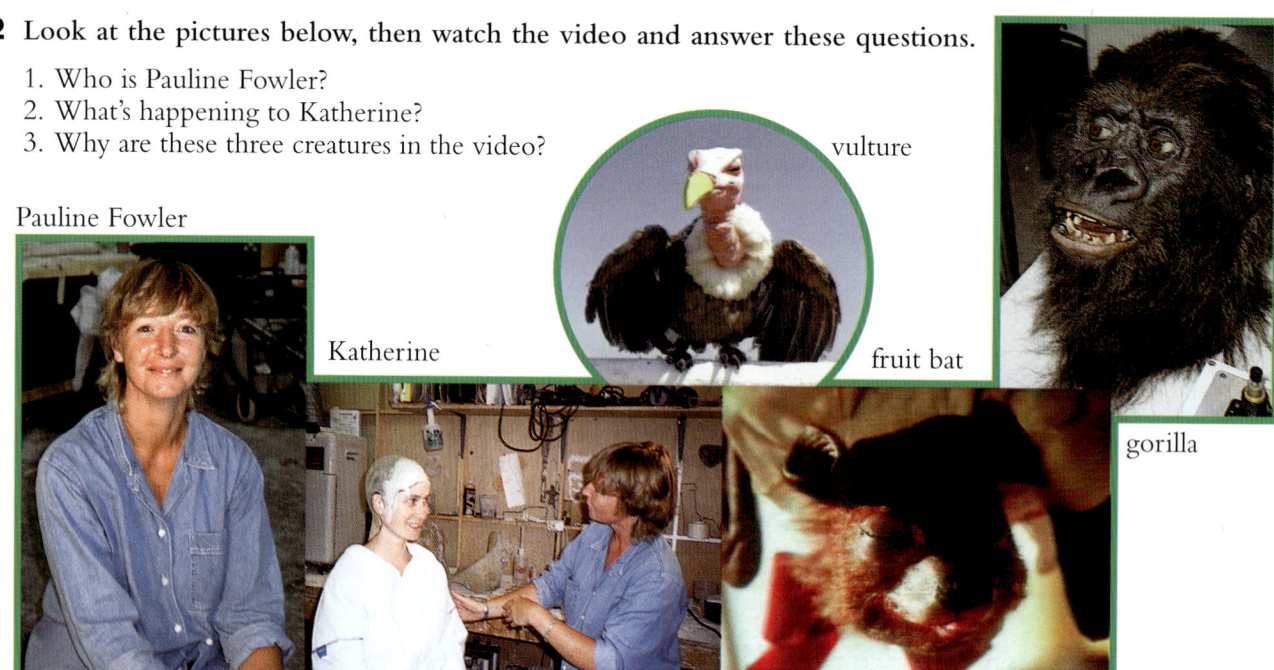

Pauline Fowler

Katherine

vulture

fruit bat

gorilla

Animated Extras

3 Read the short text, then watch the first section of the video (32:17–34:04) and correct the factual errors in the text.

Animated Extras is a company which does prosthetics and animatronics. Recently they have worked on *Frankenstein*, featuring John Cleese, and *Fierce Creatures*. When they do feature films, they usually work on them for six to eight weeks. They also make adverts, but they prefer feature films because they make more money.

Animatronics

4 Watch the next section of the video (34:05–35:33) and answer these questions.

1. What does each animal do, and what parts of the animals move?
2. Why does the first advert use a fruit bat?
3. Why does the second advert use a vulture?

Prosthetics

5 In the final section of the video (35:34–37:04), you see the process of making a prosthetic. First read these sentences, then watch the video and number the sentences in the correct order.

You remove the mask from the person's head.	☐
You now have an exact copy of the person's head.	☐
You remove the mask from the plaster.	☐
You cover the whole head with a thick liquid which forms a mask.	☐
You fill the mask with liquid plaster and leave it to dry.	☐

AFTER VIEWING

Grammar – link words and phrases

6 Now use these link words to connect the sentences from Exercise 5.

> after that   first of all   then   finally

7 Here are two more processes. Number them in the correct order then connect them using the link words and phrases above.

You rinse your hair.	☐
You dry your hair.	☐
You wet your hair.	☐
You put on the shampoo.	☐

You turn on the machine.	☐
You put your clothes in the machine.	☐
You take the clothes out and hang them up to dry.	☐
You add the soap powder and conditioner.	☐

Now write your own process using the link words.

Speaking and writing

8 The video includes two adverts which use animatronic animals to advertise certain products. Here is a plan for a new advert which uses gorillas to advertise shampoo.

1. In the first scene, we see gorilla 2 grooming gorilla 1. Gorilla 2 is very unhappy because gorilla 1's coat is in very bad condition.
2. In the next scene gorilla 3 is showing gorilla 1 a new shampoo.
3. In scene three gorilla 1 is washing his hair with the new shampoo.
4. The final scene shows gorillas 1 and 2 together again. This time, gorilla 1 looks very handsome and gorilla 2 is taking photos of him.

In small groups, think of a storyline for these animals and products.

1. elephants to advertise a family car   2. zebras to advertise paint

Write the plan of your advert and then tell the class about it.

SELF STUDY

1 The same word is missing from these sentences from the tapescript. What is it?

1. They .... models of people and animals.
2. What can you .... it do?
3. We can .... someone who's young look older.
4. To .... sure that the prosthetic moves realistically, an exact mould of the person has to be made.

Which example(s) means:

1. to produce?   2. to be/feel?   3. to cause something to happen?

2 Complete these sentences in a suitable way.

1. In my free time I like making ....
2. If you eat too much chocolate, it makes ....
3. When you leave the house, you have to make sure ....
4. I find it difficult to make ....
5. I would like a make-up artist to make me ....
6. When I go by plane, I always try to make sure ....

7

LAKE PERFUMERS

The Lake District is one of the most beautiful parts of Britain, and consequently very popular with tourists from all round the world. It is an area of natural beauty with lakes, valleys and hills with pleasant villages and small towns. It was here that John and Val Barrow, who you will see in the video, decided to start their perfume business because of the ready market of British and overseas tourists.

1 **Read the text above, then discuss these questions in small groups.**

1. What local souvenirs★ have you brought home with you after a holiday?
   What souvenirs have people brought you?
2. What are the most common souvenirs that visitors to *your* country would buy and take home?

> **Language note**
>
> ★ *souvenir*: something you buy and take home with you so that you will remember a place you have visited: for example, if you go to Mexico, you could buy a Mexican hat; if you go to Russia, you could buy some vodka or Russian wooden dolls

2 Match the sentence halves. If necessary, check the vocabulary in italics in a dictionary.

1. If you buy something by *mail order* ...
2. If you want to *set up a business* ...
3. If you don't *advertise* your product ...
4. If the *packaging* of your product is attractive ...
5. If you want to make some *perfume* ...

a. it will be difficult to sell to your *customers*.
b. you will probably need a business plan and some money.
c. it might make it easier to sell.
d. you will need the right *ingredients*.
e. it will arrive by post.

WATCH THE VIDEO

3 Look at the photos and the questions below.
Then watch the video and answer the questions.

Val

John

Andrew

Katherine

1. Who talks about how the perfume is made?
2. Who talks about packaging the perfumes?
3. Who asks about after-shave?
4. Who talks about the perfumes different nationalities like?
5. Who asks about the ingredients?
6. Who tries the perfumes?

Interview with Val

4 Watch the interview (37:50–39:54) and complete the gaps in the summary.

Val and John Barrow started their perfume business (1) .... years ago.
Before that they used to have a (2) .... They now make (3)
.... different perfumes. One of the perfumes Katherine tries smells like
(4) .... and the other smells like (5) ....
The ingredients for their perfumes come from (6) ....
They mix perfume oil with (7) .... to make the perfumes.
In the body care products they sometimes use unusual things like (8) .... or
(9) .... or (10) ....

About the business

5 Watch the interview with John (39:55–41:57) and say if these sentences are true or false.

1. Mail order is the biggest part of their business.
2. They have customers in the United States, Japan and Australia.
3. The same perfume can smell different on different people.
4. The same perfumes are popular year after year.
5. The Japanese have bought a lot of Lakes perfumes this year.
6. The perfumes are named after local places.

In the shop

6 Watch Andrew buying perfume in the shop (41:58–42:46), and complete his part of the dialogue.

SHOP ASSISTANT: Hello, can I help you?

ANDREW: Um, yes, (1) ....

SHOP ASSISTANT: Do you know what she likes?

ANDREW: No, I haven't got a clue.

SHOP ASSISTANT: You haven't any idea. Can I show you the 'White Moss'?

ANDREW: Yeah, sure.

SHOP ASSISTANT: There we are, see if you like that one.

ANDREW: Hmm, I think (2) ....
I (3) ....

SHOP ASSISTANT: A bit sweet, right. What about the er, 'Lindale Lily'?

ANDREW: OK.

SHOP ASSISTANT: Try that one. Thank you.

ANDREW: Mm. (4) .... Yeah, no, I'll, I'll have one of those, that's great. Um, (5) .... ?

SHOP ASSISTANT: We do, yes, we have them just all along this shelf here.

ANDREW: Oh right, (6) ....

Watch the video again, then with a partner read the dialogue aloud.
If necessary, listen again.

How people choose perfume

7 Watch the final part (42:47–44:02) and answer these questions.

1. According to John, what makes one perfume more expensive than another?
2. According to Andrew, why do people buy particular perfumes?
3. Does the American woman agree with Andrew?

Do you agree with John, Andrew or the American woman?
Discuss in small groups, giving your reasons.

AFTER VIEWING

Grammar and speaking – questions

8 Derek and Lucy Raymond have a small company producing hand-made chocolates. They were interviewed about their business. Look at the answers they gave, then with a partner write the questions they were asked.

INTERVIEWER: *Can I ask you some questions about your business* .... ?

DEREK: Yes, of course.

INTERVIEWER: .... ?

LUCY: Almost ten years.

INTERVIEWER: .... ?

LUCY: Well, my husband used to be a baker and I was a housewife looking after the children. When they grew up, Derek and I decided to start a business.

INTERVIEWER: .... ?

DEREK: Very little! But we learnt quickly.

INTERVIEWER: .... ?

DEREK: We produce about twenty different kinds, and only dark chocolate which is higher quality.

INTERVIEWER: .... ?

DEREK: Well, cherry in liqueur covered in chocolate has always been very popular, but we also sell a lot of chocolates with nuts in.

INTERVIEWER: .... ?

LUCY: Most of them are sold here in the shop, but some go to London and other large cities, and we do some mail order business at Christmas especially.

INTERVIEWER: .... ?

LUCY: It's very important. We always find that the chocolates in the prettiest boxes sell faster.

Now practise the conversation with a partner. See how much you can memorise together in three minutes. Then try the conversation together without looking!

9 Think of another similar product – for example, a local drink or something to eat such as cheese, a special sweet, etc. With a partner, imagine you have a small business producing this product. Think about:

– when you started the business and why
– how long ago you started it
– what you produce exactly
– how and where you sell your product
– how you package it.

Find a new partner and tell them what your product is. They must interview you about your business, as in the video and dialogue above.

SELF STUDY

Personal dictation

1 Read the interview between Katherine and John, the underlined section of the tapescript on page 61. If necessary, check any new words in a dictionary.

Read it aloud two or three times, to help you remember it.

Read it once more, and write down not more than 12 important words in the interview.

Shut your book, and try to write down what Katherine asks and John answers. It needn't be exactly the same, but must contain the main information. When you have finished, compare what you wrote with the tapescript.

Word puzzle

2 You will find all the words in the puzzle in the tapescript for this lesson on page 61. When you have finished, the letters in the black box will spell another phrase.

1. What you do to tell people about your products.
2. Not normal, not usual.
3. More than 50%.
4. You can make something less strong, often by adding water.
5. The box or covering that you put the product in.
6. The verb from *variety*.
7. You put this on a perfume bottle and it tells you the name or type.
8. *I haven't a .... means I don't know.*
9. The basic .... needed to make an omelette are eggs, butter and salt.
10. If there is only one of something, it is ....
11. A word meaning *at the beginning of a process or situation*.
12. A phrase meaning in general.
13. A shopkeeper puts products on one of these so that people can see what they can buy.
14. The people who go into shops and buy things.

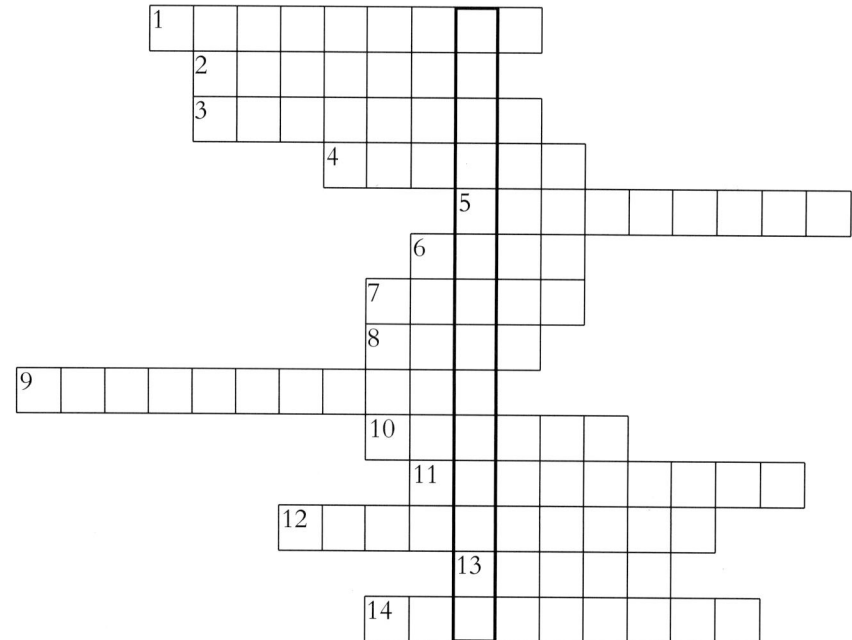

Sequence 7 LAKE PERFUMERS

8

LOCH NESS

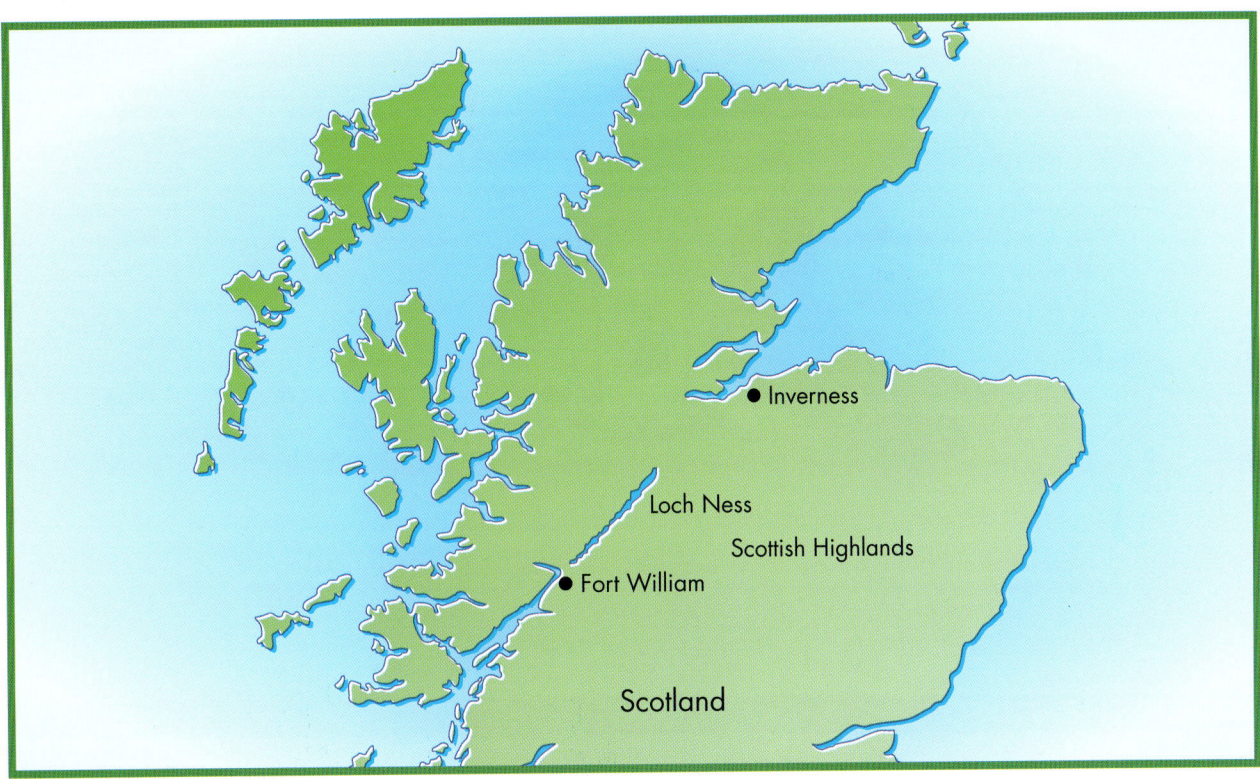

1 The map and photograph show Loch★ Ness in Scotland. What do you know about Loch Ness? What would you like to know? Discuss with a partner.

> **Language note**
>
> ★*Loch*: a Scottish word, meaning 'lake'

2 Label the objects in this picture using words from the box below.

bucket	van	kettle	waves	windmill	fishing rod	fire

WATCH THE VIDEO

3 Watch the video about the Loch Ness monster, and answer these questions.

1. Where does the first man (Steve Feltham) live and why?
2. Why does the presenter, Katherine, interview the second man (Iain Cameron)?
3. Does the video tell us definitely that there is a monster or that there isn't a monster?

The monster hunter

4 Watch the first part of the video again (44:15–46:27) and answer these questions about Steve Feltham.

1. How long has he lived near the loch?
2. When did he first become interested in Loch Ness?
3. How does he get electricity?
4. Does he always go in the loch when he wants a bath?
5. Has he ever seen the monster (or what he thinks is the monster)? If so, how many times?

Background to the loch and monster

5 Watch the next section of the video (46:28–47:08). Are these sentences true or false? If false, correct them while you listen.

1. The length of Loch Ness is 30 kilometres.
2. The depth of the loch is 240 metres.
3. There are 7,500,000,000 cubic metres of water in the loch.
4. The monster was first seen in 963 AD.
5. There have been at least 3,000 sightings of the monster.

A sighting of the monster

6 Watch the next section of the video (47:09–48:24) in which Iain Cameron talks about seeing the monster. From your understanding of the interview, complete these two sentences in logical ways.

1. One good reason to believe Iain Cameron's story is that ....
....
2. One reason why it's hard to believe Iain Cameron's story is that ....
....

Discuss in small groups.

Fact or fiction?

7 Look at these pictures, then watch the final section of the video (48:25–49:41) and complete the text below.

 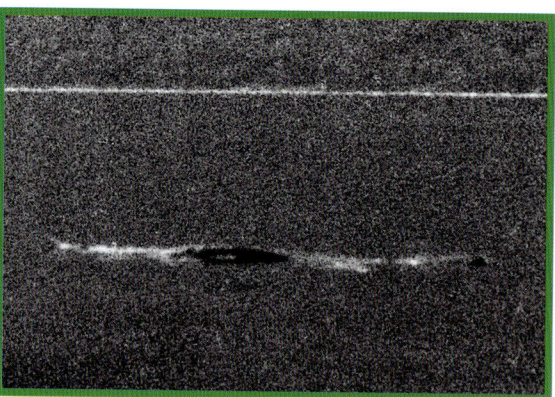

Some people say they saw a large (1) .... animal. Others say they saw something with a long (2) .... Some people even think it could be a (3) .... Scientists, however, say the monster can't exist because there isn't (4) .... So, what could it be? Two possibilities are a big (5) .... or a wave in the (6) .... Maybe there is a monster, maybe there isn't.

What do you think? Is there a monster in the loch? Do you have any similar mysteries in your country? Discuss in small groups.

AFTER VIEWING

Grammar – tenses

8 The following text is taken from the video. Underline the correct verb tense in brackets, then check your answers with the video or the tapescript.

The first sighting of the monster (*was / has been*) in 563 AD, when St Columba, an Irish saint, who (*walked / was walking*) by the loch, (*saved / has saved*) a swimmer from a large creature in the water. Since then, there (*were / have been*) over 3,000 recorded sightings.
Iain Cameron is a former policeman who (*had / has had*) an extraordinary experience in 1965.

IAIN CAMERON: I (*fished / was fishing*) for brown trout on the edge of the loch, just where we are now. I (*saw / was seeing*) an object surface.

Speaking and writing

9 You have five minutes. Imagine you saw something fantastic (a monster, a ghost, a UFO, for example). Think about these questions.

– When did it happen?
– Where were you?
– What were you doing at the time?
– What exactly did you see?
– Were other people there?
– How did you feel?
– Has it ever happened since?

Prepare your story.

In pairs, interview each other about the sighting. When you listen to someone, think of more questions you can ask them. Ask as many questions as possible.

Now write the story you heard in not more than 60 words. Show it to your partner who can correct the facts, and discuss any errors. Then read other people's stories.

A few years ago, Su Min was waiting for a bus in a country lane one evening when suddenly she saw ...

SELF STUDY

Personal dictation

1 Read the interview with Steve Feltham, the first underlined section of the tapescript on page 62. If necessary, check any new words in a dictionary.

> **Language note**
>
> ★ *to get hooked on something*: to become very interested in something so that it can become an obsession

Read it aloud two or three times, to help you remember it.

Read it once more, and write down not more than 12 important words in the interview.

Shut your book, and try to write down what Steve says. It needn't be exactly the same, but must contain the main information. When you have finished, compare what you wrote with the tapescript.

If you found this a useful exercise, you could do the same activity with the second underlined section of the tapescript.

Word puzzle

2 Complete the word puzzle using the clues and your tapescript. When you have finished it correctly, the letters in the black box should spell another phrase.

1. A place where you can stop your car by the road and park.
2. A large piece of wood cut from a tree.
3. You carry water in this.
4. The largest mammal which lives in the sea.
5. They are in the middle of your legs, between the ankles and the thighs.
6. The side of something (a road, a river, a lake, etc.).
7. Very, very interested in something.
8. A gigantic animal which does not exist now, featured in the film *Jurassic Park*.
9. Camels have two of these on their backs.
10. Very difficult, hard.
11. The place where Steve lives.
12. An animal that lives on land and sea and eats fish; their skins are valuable.
13. You boil water in this.
14. A living thing: e.g. an animal, bird, fish, etc., but not a plant.
15. You can put these in a personal stereo to provide electricity.

ANSWER KEY

1 *Possible answer*
areas: poorer area, suburbs, commercial area, residential area, downtown area
types of transport: taxi cab, tram, railway
buildings: pavement café, restaurant, department store, high-rise building, school, factory, museum, hospital
water features: river, fountain, lake

2 You can see: museums, taxi cabs, a poorer area, a tram, a river, railway (overhead), suburbs, e.g. the Stockyard area, commercial area, high-rise buildings, residential area, pavement café, school, fountains, downtown area, restaurants

3 1. food; music; architecture
2. high-rise
3. 12,000; 110; over 20 years
4. residential buildings
5. father; modern

4 1. Patricia's job
2. Patricia's first project
3. Patricia's opinion about architecture
4. Patricia's parents
5. Patricia's childhood

5 *Restaurants*: Korean, Italian, Thai, pizzeria
Music: rock music, jazz

6 2 was   3 moved   4 grew up   5 did   6 went   7 studied   8 left   9 was

SELF STUDY

2 1. bright   2. modern   3. great   4. famous   5. fortunate   6. productive   7. favourite
8. enormous   9. elegant
The word in the black box is *beautiful*.

3 A 1. E   2. B   3. G   4. A   5. C   6. H   7. F   8. D

   B 1. step out   2. behind with your right   3. clap   4. hook   5. slide   6. go forward
     7. touch the ground

4 keep fit – Barbara and Julie
have a laugh – Rhona
lose weight – Barbara
it's fun – Barbara, Andrew
you don't need a partner – Julie
you don't have to be good at it – Andrew
time goes quickly – Julie

5 1. T   2. F   3. T   4. T

6 They all think she's a marvellous teacher. They all think she makes them laugh. She
encourages them, she doesn't get angry, she's a very good dancer, she knows when some
people need more time than others.

7 *libraries*: to read, to study, to borrow books, to check information
parks: to relax, to sit in the sun, to have lunch / a snack, to have a walk
chess clubs: to play chess, to meet other chess fans
parties: to meet friends, to meet new people, to have fun, to celebrate something (a birthday,
   for example)
the beach: to relax, to swim, to do water sports, to sunbathe, to have fun, to meet friends
football matches: to see the match, to support your football team, to meet your friends
banks: to put money in, to take money out, to borrow money, to see the manager, to get
   foreign currency
airports: to travel somewhere, to meet people who are arriving, to take a friend who is flying
   somewhere (to see someone off)

SELF STUDY

2 do something well, have a lesson, stretch your arms, touch the floor, lose weight, keep fit, find
something easy, teach someone to do something

1 A Waiters and waitresses serve customers in a bar or restaurant.
Bar staff work in the bar, serving customers or clearing the tables.
Chefs cook, and some chefs order food, write the menu, etc.
Chambermaids clean the hotel bedrooms and public rooms and change the beds.
Receptionists work in reception, doing bookings, giving guests their bills, answering enquiries.
The guests are people staying in the hotel.

B A salami   B steak   C olives   D cereals   E garlic   F cabbage   G croissant
H French bread/baguette   I cold meat   J roast beef and Yorkshire pudding

3 1. 15   2. personal   3. not   4. 450   5. breakfast   6. dinner   7. 600   8. 11
9. comfortable

4 1. people from Cannes   2. the Germans and the English   3. the French   4. the Germans
5. the Italians

5 A milk, orange juice, cheese, cold meat, salami, yoghurt, jam, cereals

B 1. classic French food   2. a sandwich   3. coffee   4. well done   5. the Americans
6. cold meat

6 You must be friendly.
You must be polite.
You mustn't be familiar.
Remember! The customer is always right.

7 *Possible answers*

staff: gardening, pouring drinks, serving food, talking to customers, preparing food
guests: chatting, swimming, sunbathing, eating and drinking, helping themselves to food,
sketching or drawing, someone arriving with a suitcase
furniture/objects: bed, wardrobe, table/desk, chair, armchair, TV, lamps, curtains, chest of
drawers, pictures on the walls
breakfast table: bowls, glasses, jugs, forks

SELF STUDY

2 a three-course meal
a five-star hotel
a de luxe apartment
the night before last

Possible answers

a five-course meal
a two-star hotel
a penthouse apartment
the week before last

2 **A** A lemur B lion C deer D tiger E snake F bear G orang-utan H gorilla
I giraffe J chimp (chimpanzee) K kangaroo L camel M elephant

  B aggressive, happiness, strength, popularity, noise, timidity, dominant, intelligent, smelly

3 In the video, you *don't* see: a giraffe biting another giraffe or a snake attacking someone or something.

4 cuddle – touch
an African king snake – a Mexican king snake
many people know – not many people know
happy, mad, sick – happy, sad, sick
happy, sad or angry – happy, sad or aggressive

5 1. up to 25 2. the most productive female 3. in the centre
4. are timid, and some are in between 5. orang-utans and chimpanzees

6 *How chimps are similar to people*: Genetically 98.4% the same as humans. Like humans, they all have different characters, likes and dislikes. They have emotions like people.
A chimp called Boris: He is the dominant male, he's 31, and he's not the biggest or strongest.
A chimp called Nicky: He is very popular, very big and strong, but stupid (thick). He carries babies around which is unusual for a male.
The character of chimps: Can be angry or show compassion. They have strong friendships, especially mother and baby. They are volatile and noisy.

7 the smallest, the tallest, the most frightening, the strongest, the fastest, the most dangerous, the strangest, the friendliest (the most friendly is also possible), the most beautiful

SELF STUDY

2 ZOOSNAKESTRENGTHUNGR**Y**OUNGR**O**OMALESIC**K**INGIRAFFESCARE
DOMINANT**O**UCHUMANSTRONGORILLA

1 1. True 2. False 3. True 4. True

2 1. He did his packing.
2. They went out for a meal with some clients.
3. They went to see some old friends.
4. They checked into a hotel.
5. They went sightseeing in Prague.
6. He looked around a farm.
7. He gave a presentation to clients.
8. They went to visit his father-in-law.

3 1. He met her a few years ago in the Czech Republic.
2. He hates planes and he enjoys driving because he can see the countryside.
3. She thinks they drive too fast.
4. He thinks they drive too slowly.
5. He goes out for a meal with them.
6. He gets on very well with them.

5 sightseeing; business; at learning languages; accent is awful; help me; giving presentations; enjoy it.

6 1. We learn that Roy really likes his father-in-law, and also that his father-in-law thinks he is very musical.
2. He felt the trip had gone well; the business side was successful and he enjoyed seeing old friends.
3. He was pleased to see his dog.

8 I would like a job as a manager of a large company.
I hardly ever go out for a meal in the evenings.
I lived on a farm when I was younger.
I often go on business trips.
I'm not confident about speaking English.
I'm not good at learning languages.
I love travelling by plane.
I would love to live in a quiet village.

9 *Model answer*

I have just seen your video diary of the Czech Republic, and I thought it was very interesting. I have never been to the Czech Republic, so it was fascinating to see it on film and Prague looked really lovely. I think my favourite part was when you went to visit your friends on their farm and had a barbecue. I don't have a camcorder but I would very much like to make a video of my stay here in England. I'm sure it's more difficult than it looks.

2 1. Pauline Fowler is a Director of Animated Extras.
   2. The make-up artist is making her look as if she has a large cut on her face. This is an example of prosthetics.
   3. They are all animatronic creatures which have been used in films or television advertisements.

3 Animated Extras is a company which does prosthetics and animatronics. Recently they have worked on **Fierce Creatures**, featuring John Cleese, and **Frankenstein**. When they do feature films, they usually work on them for six to eight **months**. They also make adverts, but they prefer feature films because they **are more creative**.

4 1. Each animal is made to move in a realistic way. We see the eyes, nose and mouth of the gorilla move, the eyes of the bat and the eyes and beak of the vulture.
   2. Because the advert is for 'fruit gums'.
   3. Because the vulture is waiting for the man to die of hunger.

5 1. You cover the whole head with a thick liquid which forms a mask.
   2. You remove the mask from the person's head.
   3. You fill the mask with liquid plaster and leave it to dry.
   4. You remove the mask from the plaster.
   5. You now have an exact copy of the person's head.

6 first of all; then; after that; then; finally (*then* and *after that* could be reversed)

7 First of all you wet your hair. Then you put on the shampoo. After that you rinse your hair. Finally you dry your hair.

First of all you put your clothes in the machine. Then you add the soap powder and conditioner. After that you turn on the machine. Finally you take the clothes out and hang them up to dry.

SELF STUDY

1 make
sentence 1 = produce
sentence 2 = cause something to happen
sentence 3 = cause something to happen
sentence 4 = be/feel

Possible answers

1. cakes   2. you fat   3. you lock the door   4. friends   5. frightening
6. I sit by the window

2 1. e   2. b   3. a   4. c   5. d

3 1. Val   2. John   3. Andrew   4. John   5. Katherine   6. Katherine and Andrew

4 1. two   2. bed and breakfast (business)   3. 18–20   4. lemons   5. roses (and lilacs)
6. all over the world   7. alcohol   8. bananas   9. mangoes   10. chocolate

5 1. false   2. true   3. true   4. false   5. false   6. true

6 1. I'm looking for a perfume for my girlfriend.
2. it's a little bit sweet.
3. don't think she'll like that.
4. I quite like that.
5. do you sell any after-shave?
6. OK, great, thanks very much.

7 1. The cost of advertising.
2. They buy the ones they have seen on TV and in magazines.
3. No.

8 *Possible questions*

How long have you had your business?
What did you do before that?
How much did you know about making chocolates when you first started?
How many different kinds do you make/produce?
Which is the most popular?
Where do you sell your chocolates?
Is packaging important?

SELF STUDY

2 1. advertise   2. strange   3. majority   4. dilute   5. packaging   6. vary   7. label   8. clue
9. ingredients   10. unique   11. initially   12. on the whole   13. shelf   14. customers
The phrase in the black box is *set up a business*.

2 1. windmill   2. fishing rod   3. waves   4. van   5. bucket   6. kettle   7. fire

3 1. He lives in a van around Loch Ness because he wants to find the Loch Ness Monster.
2. Because he has seen the Loch Ness Monster (or says he has).
3. Neither.

4 1. Six years.
2. When he was seven.
3. From the windmill on top of his van (this charges the batteries).
4. Only in the summer. (In the winter he heats water and pours it over himself.)
5. He thinks he has seen it once.

5 1. False (*over* 30 km)
2. False (230 metres deep)
3. True
4. False (563 AD)
5. True

6 *Possible answers*

One good reason to believe Iain Cameron's story is that he saw the monster for 50 minutes, and other people saw it too.
One reason why it is hard to believe Iain Cameron's story is that he hasn't seen the monster again since 1965.

7 1. black   2. neck and head   3. dinosaur   4. enough food for it   5. fish   6. water.

8 was; was walking; saved; have been; had; was fishing; saw

SELF STUDY

2 1. layby   2. log   3. bucket   4. whale   5. knees   6. edge   7. fascinated   8. dinosaur
9. humps   10. tough   11. van   12. seal   13. kettle   14. creature   15. batteries
The phrase in the black box is *Loch Ness Monster.*

TAPESCRIPTS

Key to symbols in transcripts

} – indicates simultaneous or overlapping speech

[ ] – indicates interjections of another speaker

* – used in writing to represent non-standard or very informal spoken forms

---

SEQUENCE 1
POSTCARD FROM CHICAGO

NARRATOR: <u>This is Chicago. Famous for gangsters, food, music, and perhaps most famous of all for its architecture. There are many different styles of architecture in Chicago. In the downtown commercial area there are many high-rise buildings – the most famous one is Sears Tower. Twelve thousand people work here, it has 110 floors, and it was the world's tallest building for over 20 years.</u>
In contrast, if you leave the city centre and visit the smart suburbs, you can see many beautiful residential buildings. Some of them were built by the man they call the father of modern architecture, Frank Lloyd Wright.

NARRATOR: This is Patricia Saldaña Natke. Patricia is an architect. Most of her work is in urban housing, schools and hospitals. Her parents came to Chicago from Mexico over 30 years ago to look for work.
What effect does Patricia think architecture has on people's lives?

PATRICIA: I think beautiful architecture er has a very positive effect on people, and the spaces themselves transform people into happier people, more productive people also.

NARRATOR: Chicago is not all modern elegant housing for rich people. There are poorer areas. One of these is the Stockyards area, where much of the Mexican community lives.

PATRICIA: Er, this is the Stockyards area in Chicago. This is where I grew up. And I was fortunate enough to work on a project right around the corner, one of the first projects I worked on, which was a school. We were trying to capture the vibrant community, the Mexican American community here, through the use of bright colours.

NARRATOR: So what does Patricia like about Chicago?

PATRICIA: Chicago's a great city. Great city for architecture and the mix of people – all the different ethnic backgrounds and I think that brings a lot of vitality to the city.

PATRICIA: Chicago's got wonderful museums, enormous amount of restaurants that um focus on different ethnic foods. One of my favourite foods is Chicago deep dish pizza.

WAITRESS: Hi there. How are you today?
PATRICIA: Good, thank you.
WAITRESS: Great. What can I get you?
PATRICIA: I'll have a sausage and mushroom pizza.
WAITRESS: OK. What size on that?
PATRICIA: Small.
WAITRESS: Small. And to drink?
PATRICIA: A small coke.
WAITRESS: A small coke. All right, I'll be right back out with your drink.
PATRICIA: Thank you.

PATRICIA: The music is very diverse. There was a very early relationship to the jazz and blues in the African American communities. And also there are many street musicians that will play music to add some energy to the downtown area.

SEQUENCE 2
LINE DANCING

TYLER: Line dancing is the second most popular evening leisure activity in Britain. Most people think of it as an American dance, but in fact, no one really knows where it came from.
It seems to have elements of English, Irish and French dance as well.

Tonight, I'm going line dancing. I've never been before, so perhaps I should have a lesson first.
This is Heather. She's gonna* teach me. What are you gonna teach me, Heather?

HEATHER: I'm gonna teach you a dance called 'Alvara'.

TYLER: OK.

HEATHER: Right, OK, first of all, if you'd like to put your hands behind your back or you can put your hands in the front of your jeans.

TYLER: }Oh, right. Yeah, I'll, I'll do that, shall I. All right, yeah.

HEATHER: }And just let your arms be relaxed. And then the first step that we're gonna do is called a 'grapevine'. So you step out to the right, [yeah] behind with your left, [yeah] out to the right [yeah] and a touch, OK?

TYLER: A touch with? OK.

HEATHER: Just a touch with the left. Then you're going to go back and do exactly the same, [all right] step out with the left, behind with your right, out with the left, with a touch for the right.

TYLER: Right, OK.

HEATHER: That is called a 'grapevine' step.

TYLER: }That step, all right.

HEATHER: }OK, OK let's go from the beginning and … out, behind, out with a touch, and left behind, left with a touch.

TYLER: Great.

HEATHER: Got it?

HEATHER/TYLER: Right, left, right, hook, clap.

HEATHER: Bend your knees and hook behind with your right. OK, let's do that together, then, walking backward first of all. And back, two, three, hook! Forward, hook, back, hook, step, slide, step, turn, grapevine. Go straight into that. You have to turn.

TYLER: Oh, yes.

HEATHER: There is a movement [yeah?] carry on dancing, I can show you, as you go forward, you can touch the floor. [Oh!] Stretch your arms and touch the ground [OK], and back, two, three, four, forward, touch, back and step, side, step … to make it more fun.

TYLER: (laughing) Right! OK.

HEATHER: OK. Hello, my darlings! OK, you ready? OK!

BARBARA: I go three nights a week, and I go because I love it. I actually really enjoy it. In the beginning, it was to keep fit and to lose weight. I done that, I'm in my size 12 again, and it's brilliant. It's just great fun. It's wonderful.

ANDREW: Well, we come once a week, and it's good exercise, it's good fun. You don't have to be very good. You can get very hot and sweaty – I always bring my towel with me, er, to my wife's amusement and embarrassment. Um, you don't need a partner and you can learn it at your own speed, and it doesn't matter if everyone else can do it well and you can't.

JULIE: I like to go dancing, and my husband doesn't, so I can go and I don't need a partner and it's very good exercise. I don't like aerobics, it's too, too hard. I look at the hour and I think, 'when's this hour going to finish?' but with line dancing, the two hours goes really quickly. I enjoy dancing; and it's good exercise, really.

RHONA: I go because I can go on my own and um, I can, um, have a laugh, we have a good giggle and it's a night out with the girls, sort of thing.

TYLER: Do you find some dances difficult and some dances easy?

GEORGE: Well, quite a lot of them are based on waltzes, cha-chas, rumbas, things of that sort, which sort of tie in with the ballroom dancing. Er, these I like best. The faster ones, I'm not too keen on, because the legs don't work fast enough.

BARBARA: Well, I find, I think it depends on each individual. We have had older people here and they do pick it up very well. I mean, there's a 70-year-old lady here to the day and she's absolutely brilliant, so I don't think you can say that children pick it up quicker than older people. It's just, if you enjoy doing it, I think, … doesn't matter what age you are.

JULIE: When you leave school and go to work, you get out of the way of learning anything, really, and I've enjoyed that, that my brain has got to work again to learn something, you know.

ANDREW: Well, it is quite easy. It's er … not as easy as I expected and I'm not as quick at learning it as I hoped, and the girls are so much faster than the men, I notice.

ANDREW: Oh, Heather's a wonderful teacher, and she makes us laugh all the time, and, um, she's also a beautiful mover, she really is, it's just lovely watching her dance, and, er, she encourages us, makes us think we're doing very well, which perhaps we are – who knows?

JENNY: Well, I think Heather is a perfect teacher. She's so relaxed and laid back and she has a laugh um and she's um very good. She can tell when some people are taking er a bit longer to learn the dance and others aren't.

SARAH: Well, she doesn't get cross with you if you don't get it right, you know. We have a laugh about it. Some people take it, I think, too seriously and make you feel self-conscious.

SEQUENCE 3
A HOTEL IN FRANCE

TYLER: Fifteen years ago, Wolf and Shirley Rilla bought an old olive mill in Provence in Southern France and turned it into a hotel. What sort of hotel did they try and create?

WOLF: I think that nowadays people are getting tired of the big 'palace' hotels. They have their place; big five-star hotels, they are lovely, but er they're getting a bit tired of the impersonality and we wanted to create a hotel which is much more personal, which is not really like a hotel and which is more like a private house.

SHIRLEY: Every single room's different; they're all very individual. Some are bigger, some are smaller. The smaller rooms range from, I don't ... in French francs, I suppose, about FF450 per person including breakfast and dinner, and the most expensive is our de luxe apartment. I think it's something like FF600 per person per night, including breakfast and dinner, which isn't bad.

WOLF: We've only got 11 rooms altogether. We try to make them, to have a sort of, you know, Provençal touch. To feel that is ... We *are* in the Provence, and they have a Provençal touch, and we try to make them as comfortable as possible.

TYLER: Provence is a popular tourist area. So what sort of customers come to the hotel? And why?

SHIRLEY: Obviously it's tourists, um but by tourists, I mean that can be Parisians, can be people from the north of France. Actually we have people coming from Cannes, which is only half an hour away, just to spend the weekend, because in the summer Cannes can be a bit noisy. Then we have a lot of Germans and English at the beginning of the season and at the end. The French come in July and August, because that's school holidays.

WOLF: The easiest, not best, but easiest customers are the Germans, who are always happy, and always enjoy themselves, er, closely followed by the Italians, who make a lot of noise but are very amusing.

TYLER: The hotel also has a restaurant. What sort of food do they serve?

SHIRLEY: When I first came here, because I was, I'm British, they thought, 'Ah! Roast beef, Yorkshire pudding,' you know, boiled cabbage, and the French would come and say, rather patronisingly, 'I suppose this is what you're cooking', and I'd say, 'No, it's not what I'm cooking.' What we're cooking is classic French food, but mostly with a very strong Provençal angle. That means garlic and tomatoes and olive oil and olives – all the things that you associate with the South of France.

MAN: Food's really important to me – I love food. Um, and it's really so different here. In America, er you see so much fast food and er we like to experience the, um, the food of the country we're in.

WOMAN: I guess it is more of a ritualised meal where you get many courses and they're all so beautifully presented; it's more a ceremony.

DUTCHMAN: Well, I think er for the French, er lunch is very important, which in Holland is not the case. We just eat a sandwich, er have a glass of milk and that's it. Whereas when you're in er France, you always get a three-course meal at least. Er generally, I think the French er put more emphasis on the quality of food than the Dutch, which is one of the reasons that I like to go on holiday in er France, of course.

WOLF: We sometimes have problems with Americans who, er, ask for, instead of wine or whatever, they want coffee with their meals, which people find very odd, but what makes the chef totally mad is when they ask for a well-done steak.

SHIRLEY: When we started off, we did the traditional French breakfast – you know, croissants and baguettes, with 'confiture', and coffee or tea, because the French like 'tisane' which is herbal teas. People in Northern Europe tend to have more copious breakfasts, and we now have a sort of buffet-style breakfast, and we always have cheese; we have cereals, 'cause the English like cereals, and so do the Americans, but for the Americans, it's usually sugar-free, um terribly healthy-type ones, nothing with sugar; and we have cold meats because the Germans and the Dutch tend to eat cold meat or salamis for breakfast too.

TYLER: Wolf and Shirley believe in good service. But what do they think is particularly important?

SHIRLEY: The staff must not be familiar. We had a waiter here this year who really was familiar, and it was absolutely awful, and we had a lot of complaints and he had to go. He was really good, but he, he was familiar, and you can't have that in hotel staff. They must be friendly, they must be polite, but they must not be too near, you know?

WOLF: The most important thing is that, I'm afraid, the customer *is* always right, and even when he's totally wrong, he's got to be right, and people come principally to relax, so I mean, that is the atmosphere we have to create.

KATHERINE: Human beings behave and interact in many different ways. But what about our relatives in the animal world? How are they similar or different to us? And what about relationships between animals and people? I've come to Chester Zoo to talk to people who spend their time working closely with animals.

A lot of people are scared of snakes. I'm quite scared of snakes. This is Keith. He looks after the snakes at the zoo. Can I touch it?

SNAKE KEEPER: You certainly can. This is a, a Mexican king snake. They're called king snakes because they actually attack and eat rattlesnakes. Not many people know a great deal about snakes. When you work with them, if you look at them, people say how can you tell that they're happy, sad, sick or healthy. I've worked with snakes for over 30 years. I can just look at them and I know by their behaviour whether they're happy, sad or aggressive. And even this is a very, very placid snake, but if he was upset or frightened, he would bite you.

KATHERINE: Really?

SNAKE KEEPER: Really.

KATHERINE: Do the lemurs like living in family groups?

LEMUR KEEPER: Yeah, they live in um in large family groups of up to about 25, and the er the females are actually the dominant members of the group.

KATHERINE: Oh, really?

LEMUR KEEPER: So the er it's quite a strict hierarchy, and the head animal is the, is the top female.

KATHERINE: And is she the oldest?

LEMUR KEEPER: Not necessarily, no. She's usually the most productive female, probably the most fertile. When it's feeding time, you scatter the food about and the males feed on the periphery and the females are there in the centre with all the, all the goodies.

KATHERINE: Are they similar to human beings?

LEMUR KEEPER: Um, they are in many respects, yeah. They're um, you've got a whole range of personalities within the group. You've got some which are very aggressive, some which are timid, and er, everything in between.

KATHERINE: And have you become quite attached to them?

LEMUR KEEPER: Um, you, you get attached to a certain, a certain degree. But you can't form very strong bonds with them like, like you would with the larger animals – the orang-utans and the chimpanzees.

KATHERINE: Mm, because they're more similar to human beings?

LEMUR KEEPER: Yeah, so it's easier to identify with them. With the lemurs, they're, they're very much, they've got their own social group and they get on with, with their own lives. And, and they do die, so to become emotionally attached to them would be, would be very foolish.

KATHERINE: Yes. Do you get sad when they die?

LEMUR KEEPER: Um, it is quite sad when they do die, but obviously you, you can't take it too far.

KATHERINE: No, no.

CHIMP KEEPER: Well, genetically chimps are 98.4% the same as humans. Chimps are as diverse as people. Er, they've all got their own characters, they've all got their own levels of intelligence, likes and dislikes. There's a, a dominant male who's basically in charge of the group and in this group it's Boris. He's 31. Er, dominance is a combination of size, strength, popularity and intelligence. Er, Boris isn't the biggest or strongest one – that's Nicky. Er, Nicky is a very popular chimp but unfortunately he's a bit thick. Er, he's a very important member of the group: er, he carries babies around which males don't usually do. Chimps can show basically all the human emotions. Er, they have anger and dislike of each other. They also have a fair amount of compassion to each other. Mothers and infants especially, there's a lot of cuddling and kissing almost. Er, they do a lot of grooming which helps bond friendships. Friendships can last a lifetime. Er, the relationship between mothers and infants usually lasts a lifetime as well. Chimps are very volatile, er, very mouthy and noisy. Er, it's more of a challenge, I think, to control them. Er, it's a mutual respect. And I've been with them for such a long time now, you know, that I've known most of them since they were born, so it's, it's almost like my own family.

KATHERINE: And do you prefer them to human beings?

CHIMP KEEPER: Generally, yes.

KATHERINE: (laughter) Why?

CHIMP KEEPER: You know where you are with chimps.

KATHERINE: Right.

SEQUENCE 5

VIDEO DIARY: A TRIP TO THE CZECH REPUBLIC

ROY HAYES:

Hello! My name's Roy Hayes, and this is my video diary. When I was young, I wanted to work with animals in the circus, but it didn't work out, so I did the next best thing and got a job as export manager for a company selling animal feed.
My job is to travel around Europe visiting clients. Most of them are in Eastern Europe.

I went to the Czech Republic with my wife, Irena. Irena is Czech, and we met when I was on a business trip there a few years ago.
I don't like aeroplanes, so I always go by car. I prefer travelling by car because you get to see the countryside and you can stop when you want.
The only problem is that Irena and I can never agree who should drive. She thinks British people drive too fast; I think Czech people drive too slowly.

Most of my work involves meeting existing clients. They tell me what they want and I tell them what they need, and hopefully, they're the same thing.

We always go out for a meal together afterwards. I've known most of my clients for several years and we get on very well.

But it's not all business. At the weekend, we went to visit some friends of Irena's who live on a farm in a small village about 100 km from Prague. Although Irena and I live in the country, life in the country here is completely different. The Czech people I've met are always very hospitable and friendly. They're very traditional and they like making a fuss of us.

And the best bit was that I learnt the Czech word for 'sardines'!

We also went to visit my favourite city, Prague. What I like about it is the architecture and the history and it's a good chance to buy lots of presents.
I'm not sure Irena really appreciates the city because she knows it so well, but she seemed happy watching me perform in front of the camera.

Monday, and I had to get out of sightseeing mode and back into business mode. I've never been very good at learning languages. I do speak a bit of Czech but Irena tells me my accent is awful, so I get an interpreter along to help me.

I used to get really nervous about giving presentations, but I'm now pretty confident and actually enjoy it.

This part of Central and Eastern Europe is becoming very, very important for us. When the piglet is suckling, it's getting its mother's milk, it will grow quite happily ...
(*translation into Czech*)
So what we do is we process the cereals we use and we break down these starch particles into much smaller sizes so the piglet can digest them. It's a bit like ... if you had a cherry and you put it in your mouth, you could eat it, but you try putting a whole apple in your mouth and eating it!

Friday the 13th and this is the worst bit of the trip. The visit to see my father-in-law. Don't get me wrong – I really like him, the problem is, he seems to think he's Beethoven and he forces us to listen to his latest composition.

So, with that wonderful music ringing in our ears, we head for home. The trip's gone well, the business side was very successful and it was really nice to see some old friends.

Home at last, and you know what they say, a man's best friend is his dog.

SEQUENCE 6
CREATING SPECIAL EFFECTS

KATHERINE: This is Shepperton Studios, just south of London. Many famous films were made here, including *101 Dalmations*, *Alien*, *Frankenstein* and many more.
We all know about the stars in front of the camera, and we also know the names of the famous directors and producers. But what about the people who work behind the scenes? These are the premises of a company called Animated Extras. They do many different types of work for film and television. They make models of people and animals which are electrically operated and can move. This is called animatronics.

KATHERINE: This is Pauline Fowler. She's a director of the company.
What films have you worked on?

PAULINE: Oh, we've worked on an awful lot, but the ones that spring to mind I suppose at the moment is *Frankenstein* with Robert de Niro, the Ken Branagh film, and *Fierce Creatures*, John Cleese's film, which we did gorillas for, great fun.

KATHERINE: And do you do mostly feature films and television?

PAULINE: Um, we do feature films, I think, as a preference. If we can get them we will do them.

KATHERINE: Why do you prefer them?

PAULINE: Because we get, um, a long run at them – anywhere between six and eight months, which means we can be really creative.

KATHERINE: And do you do adverts as well?

PAULINE: We do do adverts and they're pretty much our 'bread and butter'. They actually pay better. They are financially better for us than on a, than a feature film.

KATHERINE: Making a model move in a realistic way isn't easy.

BOY: Kevin's taken up painting.

KATHERINE: This is an advert for a kind of sweet called Fruit Gums. And the star of the advert is an animatronic fruit bat, made by Animated Extras.

BOY: Kevin, where's the raspberry?

VOICE-OVER: Rowntrees Fruit Gums. They're very, very fruity.

KATHERINE: So this is an animatronic gorilla.

MAN: That's right. It was made for the recent film *Fierce Creatures*.

KATHERINE: Oh, yes. And what can you make it do? ... It's just like a real gorilla!

MAN: Yeah.

KATHERINE: This is an advert for rice pudding. Animated Extras had to build an animatronic vulture, which could blink.

VOICE-OVER: Hunger can put you off. Don't let it. Seize upon thick, creamy and delicious Müller Rice. And it's Müller Rice one, hunger nil.

KATHERINE: There's another area of special effects that they create and that is prosthetics. So what is prosthetics?

PAULINE: Prosthetics is um, let's see, we can make false skin. It's a, it's a kind of advanced form of make-up. We can make someone who's young look older, we can make, um, make you into an alien, we can transform you into any ... anything you want.

KATHERINE: A prosthetic is a piece of artificial flesh or skin made from a kind of rubber. Some prosthetics cover the whole body. To make sure the prosthetic moves realistically, an exact mould of the person has to be made. There are two main stages in the process. The first stage involves making a negative, rather like a photographic negative. The second stage involves making a positive mould. This is produced by pouring plaster into the negative. The rubber prosthetic is designed and made on top of the mould and then placed on the actor's face. They then put make-up on top of that.

WOMAN: There you go. See what you think.

KATHERINE: Ohhhhh. I'm not sure what my husband is going to think about this.

SEQUENCE 7
LAKE PERFUMERS

KATHERINE: This is the Lake District, a national park in northwest England. Val and John Barrow used to run a bed and breakfast. Then two years ago, they decided to do something different. They set up a perfume business here in the town of Ambleside.

Val, what did you know about perfumes when you first started?

VAL: Absolutely nothing, but we thought we'd try and find out.

KATHERINE: And you know all about perfumes now?

VAL: Yes, we learnt gradually over the last two years, yes.

KATHERINE: And how many different kinds of perfume do you make?

VAL: We have about 18 to 20 different ones, and they all come as a perfume, an eau de parfum, an eau de toilette and a fragrance spray.

KATHERINE: Can you tell me about one or two of them?

VAL: Er, yeah – er, would you like to try one?

KATHERINE: Yes.

VAL: This one is a citrus woody.

KATHERINE: Right.

VAL: I'll give it a few minutes.

KATHERINE: Mm, mm, I think it smells like lemons.

VAL: Mm, so do I.

KATHERINE: Mm, mm, it's lovely. What about another one?

VAL: Um, this one's a floral-based one.

KATHERINE: Right. Mm, that's lovely; it smells like roses.

VAL: Yes, roses and lilacs.

KATHERINE: And are you the only people who make these perfumes?

VAL: Yes, all our perfumes are unique.

KATHERINE: And where do the ingredients come from?

VAL: The ingredients come from all round the world. We actually make the perfumes up ourselves, but the basic ingredients come from round the world.
The raw ingredient is called perfume oil, and at that stage it's pure and undiluted and it smells. I'll let you smell it.

KATHERINE: Ooh, that smells horrible!

VAL: Yes, it does.

KATHERINE: And so you dilute the perfume oil with water to make the perfume.

VAL: No, we dilute it with alcohol to make the perfume.

KATHERINE: And do you use any strange ingredients in your products?

VAL: Not in the perfumes, but in the body care range, we use things like bananas and mangoes and this morning we've had an order for chocolate shampoo.

KATHERINE: Oh, people will want to drink it!

VAL: I hope not!

KATHERINE: John, where do you sell your products?

JOHN: We sell the majority within the Lake District National Park at a variety of shops and other outlets. We also have shops and other outlets in the rest of the United Kingdom and we have a mail order side to the business which includes customers both in the United Kingdom but also in North America, Australia and Japan.

KATHERINE: Do you think that people from different countries have different tastes?

JOHN: Personally, I think all people from all over the world have different tastes. Perfumes are a very personalised thing, and on two different people, the same perfume can actually smell totally different.
Each year, you tend to get a particular fragrance that has special appeal. This year, for example, 'Lindale Lily' which is a lily-of-the-valley fragrance has proved very popular with both the British and the American public, whereas with the Asians, they have tended to go for a stronger perfume like 'Langdale' and the Japanese have not been buying the perfumes, but the body care products.
At the moment, we use the 'Lakes Perfumer' label together with the names of the Lake District places that are associated with the perfumes. This is because people come to this area and enjoy their stay while they're here and it is something to take home that they can associate with the glorious area we're in.

ASSISTANT: Hello, can I help you?

ANDREW: Um, yes, I'm looking for a perfume for my girlfriend.

ASSISTANT: Do you know what she likes?

ANDREW: No, I haven't got a clue.

ASSISTANT: } You haven't any idea. Can I show you the 'White Moss'?

ANDREW: } Yeah, sure.

ASSISTANT: There we are, see if you like that one.

ANDREW: } Hmm, I think it's a little bit sweet. I don't think she'll like that.

ASSISTANT: } A bit sweet, right. What about the er, 'Lindale Lily'?

ANDREW: OK.

ASSISTANT: Try that one. Thank you.

ANDREW: Mm. I quite like that. Yeah, no, I'll, I'll have one of those, that's great. Um, do you sell any after-shave?

ASSISTANT: } We do, yes. Er, we have them just all along this shelf here.

ANDREW: } Oh right, OK, great, thanks very much.

KATHERINE: So what's the difference between a cheap perfume and an expensive perfume?

JOHN: Not a lot. Basically, all perfumes have similar sorts of ingredients, the cost of which doesn't vary greatly. The big difference in costs basically are the packaging, and the bottles that the perfumes are put in. Obviously these can be very expensive. The main factor, though, is the cost of advertising. This is what you are basically paying for with the most expensive perfumes.

ANDREW: I think that people in different countries probably do have different tastes, but I think that on the whole, people will tend to buy what they've seen advertised on television or in magazines.

CUSTOMER: I think initially, I may, may respond to the box or the label, but ultimately I'm going to really um, make a purchase, I think, based on the fragrance itself.

ASSISTANT: £12.25. £7.75.

ANDREW: } Great, thanks very much.

ASSISTANT: } Thank you, thank you. Bye!

SEQUENCE 8
LOCH NESS

STEVE FELTHAM: I was working in security for a number of years; I was always fascinated with the subject of Loch Ness and then about six years ago, I decided that, rather than just come up to Loch Ness in my spare time, I wanted to come up here full time and be a full-time monster hunter.
I remember coming here when I was seven on a family holiday, and it was then that I really got hooked on the subject. And that interest has just grown over the years.

KATHERINE: And you live here?

STEVE: I do, yeah. All the time, in the van. I move around the loch.

KATHERINE: It must get tough!

STEVE: It can do, yeah, it can do. You can get the snow up to your knees and the wind and the rain.

KATHERINE: Do you have electricity in your van?

STEVE: I do. I get that from the windmill that's on the top of the van. That charges the batteries.

KATHERINE: Uh-hm. And what about when you want to have a bath?

STEVE: Summertime, I can jump in the loch with a bar of soap, [Oh!] and in the wintertime, I can heat up buckets of water with a kettle, and then just pour the buckets of water over me, [right] yeah.

KATHERINE: Steve, have you ever seen the monster?

STEVE: I've seen one disturbance which was when I was down at the other end of the loch, watching and waiting, and something went through the waves, totally against the direction of the waves, putting up a wash as though a jet ski was going through, but with no boat, with no, no explanation as to what that was.

KATHERINE: Loch Ness is over 30 km long and 230 m deep. It contains 7,500,000,000 cubic metres of water, and somewhere, there *may* be a monster.
The first sighting of the monster was in 563 AD, when St Columba, an Irish saint, who was walking next to the loch, saved a swimmer from a large creature in the water. Since then, there have been over 3,000 recorded sightings.
Iain Cameron is a former policeman who had an extraordinary experience in 1965.

IAIN CAMERON: I was fishing for brown trout on the edge of the loch, just where we are now. I saw an object surface.

KATHERINE: And what did it look like?

IAIN: Well, in actual fact, it looked like a whale-like object. We decided that we would jump in the car. We followed it to the next lay-by. Now the whole sighting was for a period of about 50 minutes. Now, that's ... 50 minutes is a long time.

KATHERINE: And did anyone else see it?

IAIN: Yes, there was at least seven people on the other side of the loch who were, who were watching, and they undoubtedly would have had a much closer er, view of this object.

KATHERINE: And what do you think it is?

IAIN: It's very, very difficult for me to say, because I have nothing that I can compare it to.

KATHERINE: And have you ever seen it since?

IAIN: Never saw it again. Never saw it again.

KATHERINE: There are many descriptions of the monster. Some people say they saw a large black animal moving through the water; some saw a row of humps, and others saw a long neck and head.
But what could it be?
Some people think it could be some kind of dinosaur. However, several of the photos are fake, and some scientists say the monster can't possibly exist, because there isn't enough food for it. So if it wasn't a monster, what was it?
Perhaps it was a big fish, or perhaps they saw a wave in the water, or a seal, or a floating log. So it's a mystery. Maybe there is a monster, maybe there isn't.
You never know. I may be lucky!

ACKNOWLEDGEMENTS

Authors' acknowledgements
The authors would especially like to thank Andrew Bampfield, Kate Boyce, Helena Gomm and Joanne Collie.

We would also like to thank the presenters, Katherine Porter and Tyler Butterworth, and all the participants who kindly agreed to be interviewed, in particular Roy Hayes for his video diary.

The authors and publishers are grateful to the following illustrators and photographic sources:
Illustrators: Liam Bonney: p. 11; Gecko Ltd: all dtp artwork; Jeffrey James: p. 24; Mark McLaughlin: p. 42; Tracy Rich: p. 34.
Photographic sources: Martin Allen: p. 16 (salami, steak, cereals, garlic, cabbage, croissant, bread, cold meats); Courtesy of Animated Extras, Shepperton Film Studios: p. 32 *tl*, *cr*; Anthony Blake/Anthony Blake Photo Library: p. 16 (roast beef); Andrew Bampfield, Pete Kyle, Pete Ravenscroft: pp. 5, 6, 12, 13, 14, 16 (hotel, Shirley Rilla), 21, 22, 36, 37, 42, 43; Camera Press: pp. 10 *l* (Geoff Howard), 10 *c* (Stewart Mark), 44; Cinema Centre (courtesy The Kobal Collection): p. 32 *tr*; Roy and Irena Hayes: p. 27; Life File: p. 35 *b* (Nigel Shuttleworth); Nigel Luckhurst: p. 38; Christine Osborne Pictures: p. 10 *tc*; Oxford Scientific Films: p. 20 (lemur Stan Osolinski; lion Steve Turner; deer W. S. Paton; tiger Frank Schneidermeyer; snake Joaquin Gutierrez; camel David Cayless; orang-utan Daniel J. Cox; gorilla Konrad Wothe; giraffe Norbert Rosing; chimp and elephant Martyn Colbeck; kangaroo Des & Jan Bartlett; bear Wendy Shattil & Bob Rozinski); Rex Features: p. 10 *r*; Ian Robertson: p. 35 *t*; With kind permission of Roose and Partners: p. 32 *br*; With kind permission of Saatchi and Saatchi: p. 32 *c*; © STB/Still Moving Picture Company: p. 41 *b*.

t = top, *b* = bottom, *c* = centre, *l* = left, *r* = right

Design and production by Gecko Ltd, Bicester, Oxon.
Picture research by Callie Kendall

The authors and publishers would like to thank the following people and organisations for all their help during the filming of the video:
Patricia Saldana Natke, Urban Works, Chicago; Val Grove; Heather Wong; Wolf and Shirley Rilla, Le Moulin de la Camandoule, France; Chester Zoo; Roy and Irena Hayes; Pauline Fowler, Animated Extras; EMI; Nestlé; John and Val Barrow, Lakes Perfumers; Steve Feltham; Willie Cameron.

The authors and publishers would like to thank the following people for their involvement with the production of the video:
Andrew Bampfield, producer and director; Tyler Butterworth, presenter; Pete Kyle, assistant producer and sound engineer; Andrew Lovett, music editor; Paul Pearson, VT editor; Lee Phillips, assistant producer; Katherine Porter, presenter; Pete Ravenscroft, cameraman.